Getting
the
Blue Ribbon

"Getting The Blue Ribbon is perfect for leaders and those who aspire to be leaders. They have the desire to achieve more and take on more responsibility, but don't often have the foundation to manage the increased demands placed on their time and energy."

JEFF MABE, President
Premiere Properties of the Triad, Inc.

"The book is filled with simple steps and questions you can utilize to create an award winning situation."

DIANA ELY, Director, Organizational and Staff Development
Northside Independent School District

"The book made me think about how sometimes I let little things that don't affect my main goal hinder its growth and progress. Who can't stand to be reminded about something so elemental as that?"

ROBERT PONCE, Employee Development Specialist
US Department of the Interior

"Getting The Blue Ribbon is extremely beneficial to anyone who might be starting a new stage of life-whether that be college, a marriage, having a baby, or beginning a new career or promotion. Any one of these new stages can seem daunting and impossible. However, using many of the steps discussed in this book anyone can become organized and better positioned to achieve the award-winning results they are seeking in that stage of life!"

MEREDITH CARROLL, Student
The University of North Carolina

Getting the Blue Ribn

Award-Winning Results Don't Come Naturally!

Jones Loflin

ELUCIDATE PUBLISHING

Salt Lake City, Utah

Dedication

Dedicated to my wonderful wife and amazing children, whose love always brings out the best in me.

Copyright © Jones Loflin, 2011
All rights reserved.

ISBN 978-0-615-52356-9

Printed in the United States of America
Book Design by Geri Zwicky
Sketches by Lisa Loflin

LIBRARY OF CONGRESS CATALOGING IN PUBLICATION DATA

Loflin, Jones.
Getting the Blue Ribbon: Award-winning results don't come naturally/
Jones Loflin

Printed in the United States of America

10   9   8   7   6   5   4   3   2   1

For more information on products and services related to
Getting the Blue Ribbon:
1-800-853-4676 • www.yourblueribbon.com

The self is not something readymade, but something in continuous formation through choice of action.

—John Dewey

The best time to plant a tree was 20 years ago. The next best time is now.

—Chinese Proverb

A seed hidden in the heart of the apple is an orchard invisible.

—Welsh Proverb

Table of Contents

Appendix

A Surprise Visit

John exited off the interstate and turned left at the intersection. After crossing the overpass and driving for about three miles it was as if he had stepped back in time twenty years. There was no six lane highway in front of him now. The two lane road with minimal traffic gave him a moment to relax and enjoy the view around him. The rolling hills offered a picture of contrast; the oak, hickory and maple trees appeared so lifeless next to the bright green needles of the pine trees. Stopping the car for a moment on the side of the road to stretch, he took in a deep breath of the chilly fresh air as he stood up and thought, "This trip is just what I needed."

The past few years had seemed much like the interstate he just exited— moving at a frenzied pace with little time to enjoy the view.

His workload at Trendex increased constantly, making him try to squeeze more productivity out of every moment. To try to maintain a competitive edge in the medical equipment industry, Trendex frequently shifted priorities, which sometimes hampered his ability to accomplish anything to a level of excellence. Working with people from three different generations and getting them to agree on anything was tough, as well. In frustration he would sometimes say to himself, "Why can't they just see things the way I do?!"

Some of Trendex's shifting priorities impacted him in a big way. While his new position was heralded and presented as a promotion, John knew the full story. The division for which he was now responsible had been plagued by poor leadership. The company overlooked this poor performance in the past, but with the slowing economy, there were no guarantees. John knew that if he didn't improve his new division's performance, the division would be cut; he wasn't sure where that would leave him.

This "promotion" also came with a unique "opportunity" as Trendex called it. In addition to his responsibilities at the corporate office, he would occasionally be required to visit another division of the company and monitor its progress. More time on the road and managing even more people was not his idea of something better.

John's reflection about how things were growing out of control also brought him back to thoughts of his family. Being a loving spouse and parent were his top priorities, but he felt as if he were failing there, too.

He sighed and thought, "Ashley will be going to college in a couple of years and there are still so many things I want us to do as a family before she's not here every day." He could not think about Ashley without thinking about Emma. While she was only seven and spending time with her seemed less critical in light of her age, John knew that there were just some things he would not be able to experience with her as she grew older.

And then there was Amy, his amazing wife. Time with her was always too short. Her success as a teacher was well-known, but her long hours and their joint responsibilities as parents only further limited their ability to grow in their relationship. One of Amy's favorite quotes was *"Never let your memories be greater than your dreams,"* but it seemed as if they spent a lot more time reflecting on how good things used to be, before life got so crazy.

John simply felt as if his life was growing in a thousand different directions, and he was helpless to do anything about it. When the subject came up in conversations with friends or coworkers, the answer most everyone gave was, "It's just a sign of the times. We're all too busy."

That rationalization was of little comfort when he considered the consequences of not taking more control of his work and life. There was simply too much to lose if he didn't achieve more of his desired outcomes.

As he passed a Christmas tree farm with its long rows of dark green scotch pines, he reflected on how he wished his own life were a little more orderly. Where the trees were evenly spaced and growing at a uniform rate, John recognized that such uniformity did not exist for him. Some days he did seem to have it all together and things went well. More often, though, there were gaps and areas where he knew he was not getting the results he needed.

"At least this new assignment will give me two things I can look forward to: planned time out of the office and a chance to see my big sister, Tara, more often," he thought. "I've missed seeing her on a regular basis."

Tara and John grew up like typical siblings. They fought one minute and were inseparable the next. He laughed out loud as he thought about all the pranks, practical jokes, and serious moments they had experienced together.

They remained close through his college years, but began to drift apart after their parents passed away. It wasn't that they didn't want to see each other more often; it just seemed as if life kept getting in the way. Visits to one home or the other occurred about once a year, but all that was about to change.

John's work with the other division would bring him within 30 minutes of Tara's home. He would now get to see her several times a year and he couldn't be more excited. Today's stopover to her orchard would come as a complete surprise. He turned right at the "Tara's Orchard" sign and was reminded once again of her true passion as he saw the rows and rows of apple trees.

From the time she was four years old, Tara truly loved to see things grow. Their grandfather was an avid gardener and apple grower, and Tara definitely inherited his genes. She was always finding seeds and sticking them in the dirt or, as she later reminded John, "Soil. It's called soil. Dirt is what you get on your pants."

She nurtured her green thumb throughout her high school years, establishing her own roadside vegetable stand. After high school she continued to expand her operation while attending the local community college. Following graduation she purchased some land and combined it with acreage from their grandfather's farm to establish an apple orchard and commercial fruit and vegetable operation.

As he parked the car at the retail center, he noticed a couple of new greenhouses at the edge of the parking lot. "That's Tara for you," he thought. "Never satisfied with the way things are, always looking to change something." He stepped out of the car and went inside the store.

The chime sounded as he entered the store, so he knew it would only be a minute until someone came out to greet him. As he wandered the store looking at the various varieties of apples for sale, his eye was drawn to the display case along the wall. Walking up to it, he chuckled, "Let's see what she has been winning, lately." The case contained trophies, plaques, and all types of awards she had won or earned for various achievements. Her most prized possessions, however, were the long row of blue ribbons from the county fair.

He and Tara grew up in apple country. You couldn't drive more than a mile or two without seeing an orchard. From the time Tara was young she loved helping her grandfather in the orchard and entering their apples in the county fair. With the help of her grandfather she won her first blue ribbon at the age of nine. Since then, there seemed to be no stopping her. She took first place nearly every year.

His musing was interrupted by the sound of footsteps. One of Tara's employees approached him and said, "Good afternoon. I'm Rana. How may I help you?"

John put on a serious face and said, "Is the owner here?"

Rana answered, "Why, yes, she is."

"Good," John said. "I want to speak to her. I bought some apples here a few weeks ago and they rotted within a week. I expected something better for what I paid for them."

Rana seemed shocked, but held her composure. "I'm sorry you had a bad experience with our apples, Sir," she replied. "Let me get Tara so you can share your concern with her." She hurried to the back of the store, picked up the two way radio and talked in several hushed tones. John could hardly keep from breaking out in laughter as he thought about Tara and her response when she found out who he was. He didn't have to wait long.

A few seconds later Tara came scurrying through the door, drying her hands with a towel as she went to the counter to talk with Rana. John moved out of eyesight for just a moment so she wouldn't be able to see him. As Rana finished speaking to Tara, she walked up the aisle. John stepped out from behind a tall display of seed packets and Tara's tanned face erupted into a huge smile. "YOU!" she screamed. "You just never quit, do you?" They embraced and Tara quickly motioned for Rana to join them. "Rana, this is my brother, John— the world's worst practical joker."

Rana extended her hand and smiled. "We've heard some of the stories about the two of you," she said.

"I'm sure they get better with time," John replied.

"Now if you will excuse me, I need to go take care of our next crisis," Rana chuckled. "It was nice meeting you." They shook hands again and she returned to the counter.

Turning their attention to each other, Tara said, "What a wonderful surprise, John! But what in the world are you doing here? I hope nothing's wrong."

"Oh no," John replied. "In fact, I have good news—seems as if you'll be seeing more of me in the near future."

Tara smirked and said, "I thought you said you had GOOD news." Smiling warmly she then said, "I can't wait to hear about it. Can you give me about five minutes to give some instructions to some of my team members and then we can meet in the office?"

"Sure." Tara walked quickly out the back door and John went to her office in the adjacent building.

Entering Tara's office, John paused at her bulletin board. Pictures of employees and their families covered much of the space. There were wedding announcements, baby pictures and other life-related invitations. Near the center of the board was a faded piece of paper with the words, **"You are growing something every day. What grows and how it grows is up to you."** It was one of her favorite sayings.

"Good looking bunch, huh?" Tara asked as she came through the door.

"Certainly is, Sis. You've done well."

"Thanks, John," she replied. "Now sit down and tell me what's brought you back to our little corner of the world." They sat down at a small conference table and John shared more information about his promotion and the new responsibility of visiting the nearby division.

"Well, except for the extra work, that sounds like fantastic news, John. Will Amy and the kids be able to come with you?"

"Unfortunately not," John replied. "Most of my trips here will be quick hits of a day or two and then back to the main office, but I would like to carve out a day to spend here each time I come. I could really use the break. I felt my blood pressure going down the minute I drove into the parking lot."

Tara laughed. "Come back in April or August and we'll see how calm you think it is around here."

"I know it's not always slow around here, Tara," John replied, "but even in the most chaotic moments it can't be anything like what I face at work, especially now with my division possibly being cut if I don't turn things around."

"Really?" Tara said, a little hurt sarcasm developing in her tone. "You think that all I do here is plant a few seeds, manage a few apple trees and allow 'nature to take its course?'"

"No, that's not what I meant at all," John backtracked, knowing he had stirred up his sister's emotions. "I just meant that things seem to get done and done well here. I wish I had more of that same type of success in what I do more often." Tara nodded in appreciation and relaxed.

"I'll bottom line it for you. You know that display case in the store where you keep all your awards?"

"Of course."

You are growing something every day.
What grows and how it grows
is up to you.

"I look at the consistent success you have had and all those blue ribbons, and I just wish— I just wish I felt like I were winning more 'blue ribbons' in my work and personal life. So much of what I do is hurry up and finish just so I can move on to the next task. With my new position, that can't be the norm anymore."

Sitting down next to John, Tara took a deep breath and then smiled. "Snap out of it, little brother. I have no time for pity parties, especially from you. You just finished telling me they have promoted you, but you say you're not doing a good job. Something's not matching up here."

John turned in his chair. "And, that's the sad part, Tara. There is so much more I could be accomplishing if I were consistently doing a great job instead of just doing a good job. It's the same with the people who report to me. We just aren't achieving the level of excellence demanded by today's economy and the medical equipment industry. Coming here, in addition to being a good break, would give me an opportunity to be in a 'winning environment' a little more often."

"Sounds good to me, John. I'd love to see you more often," Tara replied, "but let's take it a step further. How about on each visit we spend some time working in the orchard and you can see what works for us. If you come across something of value, fantastic. If not, well, at least we've shared a few laughs and hopefully we can work a pound or two off of you." John groaned as he was reminded of his increasing waistline.

"In fact," she continued, "I'll tell you one of most important things I have learned right up front."

"Well, share. I need all the help I can get at this point."

"Choosing what you will seek to achieve a blue ribbon for is just as important as the work to achieve it. One of the reasons I have been successful in business is because I have chosen to grow award-winning apples and have planned my actions around that purpose. I could try to grow a hundred other things here, but if I did, I wouldn't get award-winning results at anything. Choosing is critical."

"Interesting," he said as he stood up to leave. "Unfortunately, on that bit of wisdom, I need to head to the airport."

Tara stood up. "Have time for one quick look into the orchard?" she asked. "It will only take five minutes."

"Sure."

"Get your coat from the car and meet me behind the two new greenhouses."

Choosing what you will seek to achieve a blue ribbon for is just as important as the work to achieve it.

Grabbing his coat, John walked toward the greenhouses. He was flooded with memories as he passed his grandfather's old hay barn. He and Tara had spent many hours as kids working, playing or just daydreaming in that old barn. As he turned to walk behind the greenhouses, Tara joined him from the other direction.

"Where are we going?" John asked.

"You'll see." They walked for another minute or so and arrived at a row of deformed and utterly strange looking old apple trees. Some were tall with only two or three towering branches while others looked more like shrubbery with an untold number of limbs zigzagging their way around the tree, almost making it impossible to identify a single branch. In some spots in the row there were only stumps where trees had once stood.

"Not exactly your best work, I would hope," John said.

"No, but they are the result of my work. These were some of the first trees I planted on my own. I was going to really show Grandpa and everyone else that I knew what I was doing, but it was during my high school years and I got busy and chose to spend my time on other things. Occasionally I would try to work on them, but eventually it was no use. I just gave up on the trees because it would take too much work to make them productive again. I knew they could not and would not produce the kind of apples I needed to sell. These trees had all the potential to produce some fantastic apples, but I missed my chance because I was too busy with other things. I keep them here as a reminder of what NOT to do if you want to get, as you say, 'blue ribbon results.'"

"So, you're telling me that I need to be more intentional about the choices I make?" John asked. "That's a little elementary, don't you think?"

"Let me finish," Tara said. "I wanted to show you that when it comes to achieving the best of anything, **letting something grow on its own doesn't always bring the desired result.** Just because you start something with good intentions doesn't mean it will turn out the way you want. And, as you can see here, it often creates something you really don't want, especially if you make the wrong choice."

Letting something grow on its own doesn't always bring the desired result.

As they turned to walk back to the parking lot, Tara's words quickly connected with his situation. These odd-looking, useless, unproductive trees were the visual examples of his current work responsibilities, growing out of control with two or three seemingly unstoppable elements. Even the tree with the mass of limbs jutting every way imaginable looked like a diagram of how he spent his time in the office switching from one thing to another. John had to admit that some of it stemmed from making poor choices.

"Makes sense to me," John said as they passed the old barn again. "It seems as if I might need to start taking more walks through my own personal and professional orchard."

"Easy there, little brother," Tara said with a chuckle. "Don't get too carried away with the language just yet. At this point we've just scratched the surface, or should I say, 'planted the tree'? There's a whole lot more to learn about growing apples— especially award-winning ones."

"Well, if there is anyone who knows anything about growing apples, it's you, Tara," John said. "Give my best to Chase."

"Yes, he will be so disappointed that he missed you, but will look forward to the next visit. Give Amy and the kids a big hug for me."

"Will do," John replied as he hugged Tara goodbye.

TARA'S TIPS

You are growing something every day. What grows and how it grows is up to you.

Choosing what you will seek to achieve a blue ribbon for is just as important as the work to achieve it.

Letting something grow on its own doesn't always bring the desired result.

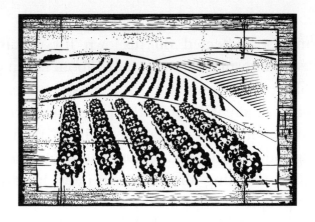

A Walk Through the Orchard

Having arrived back at work in the corporate office, John thought about Tara's words: *letting something grow on its own doesn't always bring the desired results.* Looking at his calendar for today, he could already see his schedule growing in a way that would not get him any blue ribbons. There was his weekly 9:30 Monday meeting where all of his leadership team would basically share what they had already put out in emails over the past week or given in other meetings that had taken place. Then, there was a 1:00 conference call with leaders from other divisions. It seemed as if someone was always missing from the meeting and they spent several precious minutes of time just getting others up to speed on the agenda.

John also reflected on his own list of tasks to complete. Many of them were more about maintaining something or responding to a crisis rather than improving or creating something new. He knew not every moment could be spent asking, "What am I growing today?" but at least some moments needed to be utilized thinking about ways to move his division, and the people in it, forward.

Looking outside of work, John saw that his failure to be more intentional about how he used his time often continued when he got home. He made himself available to Amy and the girls as much as possible, but he didn't always plan how to best spend the time with them.

Before getting up to go to his 9:30 meeting, John scribbled a few notes to himself. "It's time I chose to start growing something different," he thought. John moved to the conference room to await his team's arrival.

Opening the door to the conference room, John was not surprised to find Keith already in his usual seat. "Hello, Keith," he said, taking the adjacent seat, "How's your Monday going?"

"Can't complain for 9:20," he replied, "but who knows what else the day holds?"

A few moments later the rest of his team filed in and took their seats. "Good morning everyone," John began. "Good to see that you all survived without me for a few days."

There was the usual laughter and humorous comments. "As you know, I'll be gone to the other division for a couple of days every few months.

"Normally, we begin our meeting with updates from each of you, just like other managers in the past have done, but today I want to do something different. He went to the whiteboard and wrote the question: "What will you grow today?" His team gave him a confusing look. He verbalized the question: "What will you grow today by your efforts?"

Michelle spoke up. "I've got a new marketing idea I want to develop for one of our new products." Slowly, other members of his team responded with various projects they were working on and ideas they had about potential tasks to undertake.

"Good," John replied. "I'd like for all of us, myself included, to take a little different attitude toward our work day. I think too often we just allow our work to take its own course without giving much thought to what the end result actually should be or what choices we are making. As you know, the stakes are higher for all of us now if we want this division to start getting better results."

John and his team spent the next few minutes reviewing their goals and clarifying how various tasks being undertaken by everyone would contribute to achieving those goals. The discussion was moving along well until Josh spoke up. "So, what should I expect to do differently with this 'new' way of working?"

Before John could respond, Keith answered Josh's question. "The difference for me is that I'll prioritize the things that will help me best 'grow' the results I am expected to create as an employee and we are expected to achieve as a team."

"Exactly, Keith," John responded. "It's about being more intentional in working on those things that will give you the best results. It's about choosing to work on them first and not last." Josh nodded slowly in agreement. After wrapping up a few administrative details, John ended the meeting.

Over the next few weeks, John frequently caught himself asking, "What do I need to grow today?" and found the question useful in determining what might need his attention. Options could be anything from an assignment he had given to one of his staff that now needed to be brought to a close, or simply reviewing reports from past quarters. He also recognized that with his workload he had also neglected some of his team members and they were, in Tara's words, growing in a way that wasn't creating the results he or Trendex wanted.

John also tried to be more deliberate about his time away from work. He started looking at different meetings and responsibilities he had in the evenings and planned activities with Amy, the girls, or some of his close friends around those obligations.

Another result of his talk with Tara was asking himself two questions at the end of the day:

- "What did I grow today?"

- "Will I like the end result of what I grew today?"

This daily ritual gave him a way to reflect on his work and interactions to see if he were moving things in a positive direction or falling back into his old habit of allowing things to grow out of control.

Ultimately, John recognized the value of being more intentional with his schedule. It had become easy for him to just stay crazy busy, but that wasn't getting him the results he knew he was capable of, or the results that Trendex expected. To help him better manage his workload, he either wrote, "Done" or "Done Well" next to each task on his list. For the ones that needed to be "done well," he tried to schedule them when his physical and/or mental energy was most up to the task. For the tasks that simply needed to be "done," he would place them in his schedule where they would best fit with everything else.

In a couple of weeks he would be on the road again, visiting the other division. He looked forward to seeing Tara and learning more about her wisdom gleaned from growing apples.

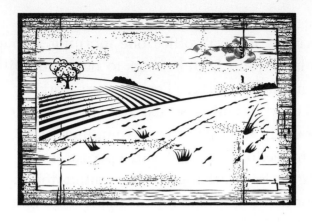

Working at the Source

John's next few weeks were hectic ones. The idea of being more intentional was working, but it was not easy. The other managers before him had simply gone with the general flow of things and had not tried to make any meaningful changes.

Fighting for blocks of mental focus time was challenging, especially with the increased demands from his team members at work. He tried to learn as much as possible about the division's performance in the past to get some direction for the future.

Some of the personal changes John desired to make also seemed to be at a standstill. He wanted to spend more quality time with the girls and with Amy, but he still could not find a way to make his planned activities become a reality. Knowing he would be visiting Trendex East in a few days, John hoped his time alone with Tara would offer some insights on what to do next.

Arriving at Tara's office one morning a couple of weeks later, John found things to be a little different than on his last visit. People were working in the greenhouses planting seeds, and he could see other employees in several of the surrounding fields.

"Why, hello," Tara said with a playful smirk. "As you can see, we're just hanging out, waiting for the seeds to plant themselves and for the apple trees to grow on their own."

"Okay," John retorted. "I get the picture. I was wrong when I said that things aren't busy here. Forgive me."

"That's okay, John. We know you're new to this 'growing thing,'" Tara replied. She gave him a wink and said, "Let's get started." They walked to one of the storage buildings behind the office.

Tara handed John a pair of gloves as they began unloading some bags of fertilizer from a truck. "Is all this fertilizer for your apples?" John asked.

"No. These bags are for the vegetable plants; those are for the strawberries, and the smaller bags are for the flowers we grow in the greenhouse."

"Why so many different ones?" John asked as he put the last bag on the stack.

"I'll explain as we take these bags of fertilizer for the apple trees to the upper orchards. Hop in the truck." John went to the other side, hopped in, and closed the door as they started down the gravel road.

Tara began: "Trees will attempt to grow in almost any environment. As long as they get the minimum requirements of water, nutrients and light, they will grow to some degree. They just won't grow at the desired rate or produce the quality or amount of fruit we need to make them profitable."

"So, the fertilizer provides what is missing?"

"To a degree," Tara answered, "as long as the limiting factor is nutrient-related. If the limiting element is water or soil-related, the answer probably wouldn't be fertilizer."

"But let's say the problem is nutrient-related," John continued. "How do you know what fertilizer to use?"

"We just guess," Tara answered with a chuckle.

John rolled his eyes and said, "Okay, smart girl. Really, how can you tell?"

"I'll tell you after we get these bags unloaded for Ryan to use on these trees," Tara said. She stopped the truck, and they got out and unloaded the bags.

After they finished, Tara rested on the side of the truck and continued the conversation from a few minutes earlier. "To answer your earlier question, I have data from years and years of research and experience about what the nutrient requirements are for optimum growth of almost any plant. I review that information with my team members to give us an idea of the ideal growth environment.

For plants grown in the greenhouse we can pretty much create the perfect combination of light, temperature, soil, water and nutrients, but for plants grown in the field, like apple trees, we can't recreate the perfect conditions."

"So, if you can't create the ideal environment for a plant, why grow it?"

"Just because I can't create the ideal environment doesn't mean I can't produce a quality result," Tara answered. "The perfect environment for growth rarely exists. **In the absence of an ideal environment, you must determine what you can and can not control.** If we always had to have the perfect conditions, we wouldn't grow anything.

"Once the basic elements of water, light and soil are taken care of, we have to determine what combination of nutrients is best for the plant." Tara pointed to the bags of fertilizer on the pallet. "See the numbers '10-10-10' on the bags?"

"Yes."

"Those numbers indicate the amount of three key nutrients in the bag— Nitrogen, Phosphorus and Potassium," Tara continued. "Some plants require a different amount of one nutrient or another to grow best. While these are the big three, there are a number of other nutrients that plants need to absorb through the soil if they are to produce the desired result.

In the absence of an ideal environment, you must determine what you can and can not control.

"The key thing to remember is that **a tree will only grow as fast as its most limiting nutrient.**"

Tara's comment struck a chord with John. "So I can provide an overabundance of one nutrient, but if it is lacking a critical amount of another nutrient, I won't get the desired result?"

"You got it," Tara replied. "You are just wasting your resources."

As they drove back, John looked out across the rolling hills. Tara's explanation helped him understand his own "growing" dilemma. He had never taken the time to really examine what his ideal work environment would look like and what was needed to create it. He also had not identified the critical "nutrients" needed for success in some of his recent tasks or how he could supply them for himself or his team. Consequently, many of his results were good, but certainly not worthy of a "blue ribbon."

A tree will only grow as fast as its most limiting nutrient.

Her comment about "perfect conditions not existing" struck a chord with him, as well. He thought back to a weekend getaway he had recently planned for Amy and himself. An obligation at church had prevented them from being away for two nights, so John cancelled the trip. Thinking about Tara's comment helped him realize that even a trip away for one night would have been beneficial to their relationship. Months had now passed, and they still hadn't found a time to make it work.

Pulling up to the office, Tara said, "Walk with me for a moment." They walked to a greenhouse containing some strange looking plants. "Ever seen these before?" Tara asked.

"Not sure," John replied, "but, they do look familiar."

"These are hydrangeas. Some people call them snowball bushes because they have big ball-shaped flowers on them."

"Yes!" John said. "Grandma Gert used to have some of these at the corners of her house. They were pink, if I remember correctly."

"Yes, that's right, but did you know that some actually have blue flowers?"

"Are the pink ones girls and the blue ones boys?" John chuckled.

"Ha, ha, very funny. No, what makes the plants have different flower color is the type of fertilizer. One type causes them to have blue and another one produces pink flowers. A different combination of inputs gets a different result." They turned and headed back to the office.

"I'm still confused about one thing," John stated.

"What's that?"

"I will admit that I don't get all of this planting, growing, orchard thing. But, a minute ago you mentioned that when planning for tree growth you determine the optimum growing conditions, and then create the best environment possible. I understand that in a greenhouse your soil comes in a bag, but how do you know what's already in the soil? Don't some soils already have nutrients in them? I seem to remember that red dirt has lots of iron in it, right?"

"You were awake that day in chemistry class," Tara said with a chuckle. "Yes, certain soils, or 'dirt,' as you want to call it, do already have some nutrients or elements present in them. To make sure, we only add what is needed. Obviously, we have to test them. Come to my office for a minute."

Walking into her office, Tara shuffled through a stack of materials on top of her conference table and produced a large sheet of paper with lots of numbers. At the top it read *Soil Test Results.*

"These are the results from a test on the upper orchard soil. If you look across the page, you will see what nutrients are needed and in what amounts each should be added to the soil. Taking a soil test helps ensure that we don't add too much or too little to the soil. Making a mistake could be very costly when you're talking about all the apple trees I have up there." She showed him a couple more reports for other fields where various plants were to be grown. Soon it was time for John to head to the airport.

"Well, Sis, I need to be on my way," John said.

"Oh, don't leave, John. We haven't even begun to talk about macro and micro nutrients, photosynthesis or even transpiration. I thought you wanted to know everything," Tara said with a grin.

"I've had enough for one day," John said, touching his hands to his head. "My brain hurts from all this learning. I'm beginning to think what I do may be easier than managing this orchard. I do see how I need to do a little more work on the 'growing side.'"

Tara pointed to her favorite sign and said, *"You are growing something every day. What grows, and how it grows is up to you."*

With a quick hug, John walked to his car and headed to catch his flight.

TARA'S TIPS

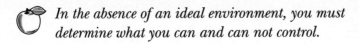

In the absence of an ideal environment, you must determine what you can and can not control.

A tree will only grow as fast as its most limiting nutrient.

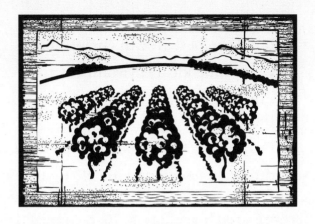

Supplying the Nutrients

John's flight home gave him a chance to digest his day with Tara. He was sure he would flunk a test about plant growth and nutrition, but he could see the parallels to improving his own situation, and getting a better result. He wrote in his pad:

- Trees will attempt to grow in almost any environment.

- In the absence of an ideal environment, you must determine what you can and can not control.

- A tree will grow only as fast as its most limiting nutrient.

- To build the best growth environment:
  - Determine ideal environment.
  - Evaluate current conditions for resources that exist.
  - Provide the right combination of nutrients.
- A different combination of inputs gets a different result.

John considered his situation. He recognized that he had been so busy that he had not really taken a moment to outline the ideal environment to get better results. He had come up with a list of things to do, which related to his priorities and goals, but not ways to nurture the completion of those items and help them grow to their full potential. He spent a few minutes outlining the key "nutrients" needed to be more successful. For his personal and family life he included:

- Developing more specific goals related to getting the blue ribbon as a spouse, dad, and friend

- Better awareness of Amy, Ashley, and Emma's schedule each week

- Identifying the time required for personal projects or interests and prioritizing them so that I can see where they might fit within my schedule

For work he listed:

- More uninterrupted time at work

- More individual time with each team member instead of frequently trying to meet with them as a group

- Listing current projects and "next steps" and reviewing them more frequently to see opportunities to move each project forward.

He then thought about how and where he might find or create these resources. John sat back and thought about his team members at Trendex, as well. "They want to be successful. They are just struggling because something is missing. I need to figure out what is limiting their efforts." He decided to meet individually with each of them when he got back and ask them three key questions related to their work environment.

As the plane landed, John gathered his belongings and headed to his car.

Michelle was the first person John met with after returning to the office. He knew she was struggling more than the other members of his team. Walking into her office, he asked her how things were going.

"Okay, I guess," was her reply. "After our 'growing' meeting a few weeks ago I was excited. I focused on some items I needed to make a priority, but things have stalled. I keep trying to do things differently, but I fall back into the same routine."

John looked at Michelle and said, "Don't be so hard on yourself. I'm partly to blame. I should have given you more guidance and support when I asked you to be more intentional about your priorities. The good news is that you have survived and it's time to get things growing."

"I think you mean 'going' don't you?" Michelle said as she chuckled.

"No, actually I do mean growing," he replied. "Let me ask you a question. What would be the ideal environment for you to be able to produce better results?"

Michelle sat back in her chair for a moment and said, "Hmm... a few less meetings would help. That would give me more time to focus on getting actual work done, and doing it well."

"Good start," John responded. "What else?"

"The chance to say 'No' every once in a while," Michelle stated. "Every time I think I am getting a handle on things and can make some good strides toward improving things in my group, I get asked to be on some planning team or take on something else. I really need some room to get my own group turning out better results before I get involved in anything else."

John had not expected this second response from Michelle. He had thought she wanted the additional opportunities and never realized that they were actually hindering her from accomplishing her core responsibilities well. He made a few notes and then asked his second question. "What would you say is the most limiting factor to making this work?"

Michelle looked away for a moment and then replied, "That's a tough one. The easy answer would be 'time' but I think the better answer is 'Trendex's willingness to accept the fact that things could get worse before they get better.' Anytime you create a change there's a learning curve for everyone and that can diminish productivity."

After making a few more notes, John spoke: "Michelle, I appreciate your honesty. It's one of the things I have come to admire about you. I was going to ask you a question about what I could do to help create this environment for you, but I already have some answers. I'll check with the rest of the team and see if we can shorten our weekly meetings and also try to improve our communication by email. If we can establish a guideline for weekly updates from everyone, we can avoid having to meet and listen to everyone's reports at one time. As for not adding to your work list, I'll try to do a better job of spreading the assignments to others in the office.

"As for the need for Trendex's understanding about a change in productivity, there's not a lot I can do about that, mainly because the shareholders are so sensitive about any changes in productivity. What I can do is talk with the executive team and let them know that they might see a decrease for a while, but to assure them that better results are coming. Would that help?"

"Absolutely," Michelle replied. "That would relieve some of the pressure I've been feeling lately. And, I might even be able to produce a few more 'blue ribbon' results."

John chuckled. "Hey, you have been listening haven't you? I wasn't sure if my 'apple orchard talks' were working or not."

"Oh, it's been good for me," Michelle replied. "I find myself often asking, 'What did I grow today and will I like the results in the future?' If the answer to the second question is 'no,' I look at what I might need to do differently tomorrow or the next week."

John rose as he gathered his materials. "Thanks for the encouragement, Michelle," he replied. "I'll pass the kudos on to my sister." Michelle smiled in approval as John headed out the door.

John laughed to himself as he returned to his office. "That's one more chance for blue ribbon results." He sat down at his desk, made a few more notes about the meeting and turned to his next task.

Unexpected Growth

After his talk with Michelle, John spent more time thinking about his own situation. *A tree can only grow as fast as its most limiting element will allow,* he recalled to himself. Procrastination was one of his most limiting elements in being successful with many of his major tasks and projects. He was excited about what the end result could bring, but allowed himself to get overwhelmed with the details, and sometimes lost his motivation. He decided that the answer to his procrastination was to tell more people in his "inner circle" about what he wanted to do to keep him accountable. He also set smaller, more obtainable goals for himself that prevented him from getting overwhelmed by always focusing on the end result. Lastly, he forced himself to finish what he started, even if the results weren't always as good as he had envisioned. "I don't have to get a 'blue ribbon' in everything," he reasoned.

As the weeks passed, he began to see positive results. Michelle implemented a number of the changes she wanted to make in her department, resulting in her first month of increased productivity. John's recent meeting with Matthew identified some opportunities for improvement, as well. Josh, Luke, and Chris were experiencing better progress as a result of John's three-question meeting with them, too.

On a personal level, John also found success: For months he and Amy had been trying to find time for a daily walk together. When they discussed answers to the three questions, they realized the most limiting factor was Emma. With Ashley's busy schedule she wasn't always able to look after her while they were gone. They enlisted the help of a neighbor who was more than happy to keep Emma while they were taking a walk. The uninterrupted conversations with Amy were wonderful. For a brief moment, John thought he was on the way to his first quarterly "blue ribbon" results, but he was soon reminded there was more to learn.

It started with Keith. He stopped by John's office one day and announced that he was planning to retire in the next year. Keith had worked so hard to keep things running smoothly in his division, but told John he thought it was time to think about slowing down. John kicked himself for not recognizing the potential for this to happen. Keith had even mentioned he was thinking of retiring some time ago. He really needed Keith's knowledge of the company and products right now.

Chris was the next person who needed extra attention from John. Despite his easy going demeanor and ability to get the best out of his team members, he was running into problems. Success in his department meant the hiring of three new people and getting them up to speed, which was proving more challenging than expected.

John was also not immune from these new challenges. The increased demands on him had reduced his focus on his physical health and he was once again gaining weight... and he had a half-marathon coming up in just six weeks.

Needing to get another perspective, John called Tara. When Rana answered, she told John that Tara was out in one of the fields, but that she would have her call him when she came back. About an hour later, his phone rang. It was Tara.

"Wow! Things must really be crazy around there, or did I disturb you from your morning nap?" John chided.

"Oh yes. In fact, let's make this short. My afternoon nap is coming up soon." In spite of her teasing tone, Tara's voice sounded tired.

"Just kidding, Sis. This is your busy season, right?"

"You'd better believe it. What's up with you? I haven't seen you in a few weeks. It seems as if I may not be the only one who is busy."

"Well, that's why I'm calling. You got me into this mess, and now you need to get me out," John said with a hint of sarcasm and humor.

"What in the world are you talking about?" Tara responded.

"When you and I started this whole 'apple orchard' journey, you taught me about being intentional and making better choices. I realized that my less than stellar results were due in large part to a lack of focus on my desired outcomes. You then showed me that I needed to create the right environment for my plans to grow and be successful. That works, too."

"I thought you said I had gotten you into a mess, Tara said. "Right now it sounds as if I should be expecting one HUGE Christmas gift from you this year."

"Yes, except for one thing: Focusing on growth has caused more challenges to pop up than ever. It seems like the more growth happens, the more obstacles and distractions appear around me and my team."

There was a long silence on the phone and then Tara said, "Weeds are trying to take over, aren't they?"

"Weeds? What are you talking about?"

Tara said, **"The same environment that creates opportunities for optimum growth also creates the ideal environment for weeds to grow.** Weeds steal resources that could be used for the tree. They can ultimately limit your harvest of apples or any other fruits or vegetables."

The same environment that creates opportunities for optimum growth also creates the ideal environment for weeds to grow.

"Okay, so I have weeds," John responded. "But with these types of weeds I can't just go to the store and buy some type of spray and kill them."

"No, but you can take steps to prevent them from becoming such a problem in the future. Remember the day we put plastic down just before planting the strawberry seedlings?"

"Sure."

"While the plastic helps with moisture retention for the roots, it also keeps weeds from growing around the plants because it takes away their ability to get light. For our apple trees we take a different approach. We may go through the orchards once a month and spray around the trees. For our organic apple tree production area, however, we might use mulch, grass clippings or something else to limit the weed's ability to grow. Whatever the situation, it's important to remember that **preventing the weeds from growing is much more effective than trying to remove them later.**"

Preventing the weeds from growing is much more effective than trying to remove them later.

"You got that right," John said. "Tara, thanks for listening. Sorry if I was a little over the top when I first called. I really have benefited from our discussions."

"I know you have, John. Just remember that growing award-winning apples or achieving outstanding results in anything of value is not easy. If it were, everyone could do it."

"Thanks," John replied. "Talk to you again soon."

As he put down the phone, John thought about the concept of weeds. He even drew a picture of an apple tree, and around its base, he listed some of the things that were attempting to take up resources he needed to get the outcomes he had identified. They included:

- Increased mistakes created by a faster pace in his division

- More demands on time normally spent for personal growth and well being

- Trendex's acquisition of another medical equipment company

As he reviewed the list, John remembered Tara's previous tip about identifying what you can and can not control. He knew that Trendex's acquisition was something over which he had no control, and he would just have to manage any additional activities related to the acquisition as best as possible. As for potential increased mistakes, John thought about creating some brief checklists that everyone on his team could use to help minimize the potential for missteps, but still keep moving at a fast pace.

To better manage the increased demands on his personal time, John made a list of "critical tasks" related to his personal well-being. They included items like "morning exercise" and "taking time away from work during lunch." John knew that while these activities were a part of his personal orchard, they were instrumental in helping him get better results at work. With his weed management plan beginning to take shape, John moved on to his next task.

TARA'S TIPS

The same environment that creates opportunities for optimum growth also creates the ideal environment for weeds to grow.

Preventing the weeds from growing is much more effective than trying to remove them later.

Looking at a Different Type of Apple

Leaving the airport, John was eager to get to Tara's place. Because of scheduling, he would be visiting Tara first and then heading to Trendex East the next day. Arriving after dark, he pulled into her driveway and got his bag out of the car. He was met at the door by Chase.

"Hey, it's the new hired hand," Chase exclaimed. "Hope you're ready for some hard labor tomorrow."

"Work?" John retorted. "I come out here to get away from work."

"That's not what Tara said. You'll have to take that up with her." He took John's bag to the guest bedroom, and Tara emerged from the kitchen to hug John.

"Ready to go at it, tomorrow?" she asked.

"I guess. More fertilizer to move?"

"Not exactly," she said. "I don't want you to think that everything we do at the orchard is easy. Blue-ribbon-apples do not just happen on their own."

"You know, I'm beginning to understand that statement a little better," John replied. "It seems as if I'm spending more time intentionally taking stock of how things are going and looking for ways to create a better environment to get things done."

"Funny you should mention 'stock,'" Tara stated. "Tomorrow is all about stocks and scions."

"What?"

"Oh, never mind," Tara said with a shrug. "We'll have plenty of time tomorrow to discuss such things. How about some dessert before we call it a night?"

"Depends on what you have," John said with a grin.

Chase yelled from the kitchen: "You know she only makes one dessert for you—apple crumble."

"In that case," John replied. "I'm in."

"I thought you would be," Tara said with a chuckle. They moved to the kitchen for John's favorite treat and later headed off to bed.

After breakfast the next morning John and Tara went to the orchard. The sun was shining brightly and the feel of spring was in the air. They joined two of Tara's employees and drove up to a newly developed area of the orchard. John strained to see any apple trees and said, "I thought we were working on apple trees today. Is this another one of your practical jokes?"

Tara replied, "No. I don't have time for such things today. We need to get this grafting done before the growing season kicks into high gear." The truck came to a stop and Tara's employees began laying out some strange looking knives and short sticks on the tail gate of one of the trucks.

"This looks more like surgery," John said. "What in the world are we going to do?"

"I told you. We are going to be doing some grafting."

"Okay," John replied, "But WHAT is grafting?"

"Grafting is a process where you take the strengths of two different things and create a better result," Tara began. "There's a new variety of apple that doesn't naturally grow in this area. Its roots don't perform well in this type of soil. With grafting I can take a piece of the stem from this new type of apple and graft 'or connect' it to the stem of another type of apple tree and grow those apples here."

"I'm still not sure I follow you, Tara," John replied. "Connecting two pieces of different trees together?"

Grafting is a process where you take the strengths of two different things and create a better result.

Tara opened the door of the truck and took out a notepad. She drew a picture of the grafting process, labeling the individual parts so that John could better understand how it worked. Once she finished her explanation, they walked to the first row of young trees where her employees were working. "Watch what Ryan is doing," Tara said. John observed as Ryan gently cut a small section from the stems they had brought. He then cut a "T" shape in the bark about six inches from the ground on the trees that were already planted and then slid the small piece of stem underneath the bark on the tree where the cut was made. He then repeated the procedure on the other side of the stem and secured the grafts with flexible bands.

"That looks hard," John said, admiring Ryan's work.

"It is difficult," Tara replied. **Changing something that is established is rarely easy, but it is necessary if you want to get something better.** There are so many things that can go wrong to cause the graft to fail. We won't even know if these grafts are successful for a few months."

Changing something that is established is rarely easy, but it is necessary if you want to get something better.

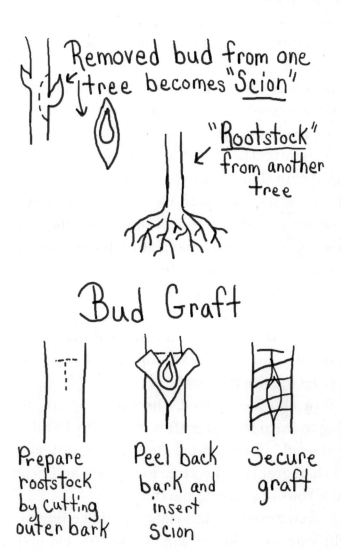

Removed bud from one tree becomes "Scion"

"Rootstock" from another tree

Bud Graft

Prepare rootstock by cutting outer bark

Peel back bark and insert scion

Secure graft

"Then why go to all the effort if you know it may fail?" John asked.

"Because achieving the best of anything requires being willing to change and sticking with it," she replied.

Tara didn't know it, but she had pinpointed one of John's biggest obstacles to getting better results— being willing to change. He was okay with small changes like the ones he had been making so far, but to lead or guide a significant change or to make one himself was way out of his comfort zone. With the situation at Trendex and his desire to improve things in his personal life, John knew his resistance to change was not serving him well.

Tara walked back to the tail gate with the knives and stems and attempted to give one of each to John. "Okay, it's your turn," she said.

"I don't think so," John answered, motioning with his hands. "I'd hate to kill all these trees. You would never let me live it down."

Tara chuckled. "Well, the only way you are ever going to learn how to graft is to actually DO it. So, let's get started." Tara handed the knife and stem to John and then grabbed the same for herself and headed off to the rows of young apple trees.

John realized she was right about needing to try the technique so he joined her in the row. He had to ask for assistance from Ryan or Tara on several occasions, but soon he was beginning to pick up on the process.

Tara inspected his work from time to time, congratulated him on his efforts and sometimes offered advice on how to improve his skill.

After a couple of hours, the excitement of learning something new gave way to fatigue of the back. All this bending and kneeling had John ready to call it a day. He was quite relieved when they finished the last row of trees and even more excited when Tara mentioned lunch! She took a cooler from the back of the truck and offered him a sandwich.

"Fine dining today, I see," he said with a grin.

"Only the best for my brother," she retorted. They sat on the tailgate of the truck and began eating.

"Enlighten me a little more about grafting," John began. "It's a fascinating process, but I could see where it would be so important to only use it when absolutely critical."

"That's for sure," Tara replied. "When you consider the investment of resources needed to make grafting successful, you have to choose wisely."

"So, how *do* you choose when to create some grafted trees and when to keep using the standard ones?"

"Do you remember what I called the bottom part of the graft that has the roots?" Tara asked.

"Woodstock, I think," John said with a chuckle. "No. I think you called it the rootstock."

"That's right. When contemplating a possible need to create some grafted trees or really to make any kind of significant change, I like to take 'stock' of the situation by asking myself three questions."

"And you're going to share those with me, right?"

"It will cost you," was her reply.

"Put it on my bill," John mused.

"The first question I ask," Tara began, "is, 'What do I know?' For example, if one person each season asks about a type of apple I don't currently grow, that doesn't indicate a need to grow it; however, if ten people in one season ask for a certain type of apple I don't offer, I'd better get started doing my homework. I look at trends in the industry, what other growers are producing and any other factual information that will help me make a decision.

"Once I have that question answered, I move on to the second one which is, 'What do I *think* I know?' I've been in this business a long time and seen a lot of things change. A few years ago several of my friends who have orchards laughed at me when I talked about the need to find alternatives to chemical pesticide use. They said it would go away. The interest in pesticide-free fruit did not go away, and the number of apples that I sell that are organically grown increases every year. I can hardly keep up with the demand. I might also consider how many of these grafted trees I could sell to other orchards or even in the retail center to people who want these trees for their home."

"So, answers to the second question are more—from your gut?" John asked.

"Right," Tara answered. "Too often we discount our own insights and experience. We are afraid of what they are trying to tell us. **Always basing your change on what you think you know is dangerous, but when you reconcile it with what you know, a clearer answer begins to emerge.**"

"I thought you said there were three questions," John responded, somewhat perplexed. "It would seem to me that you have all the information you need to make a decision about a change."

"Not quite. Your decision would be based on some solid thought, but to help clarify the choice even more you have to ask the question, 'What do I not know?'"

"Now you're sounding like the Cheshire Cat from *Alice in Wonderland*," John said with a laugh. "That's a riddle— not a question."

*Always basing your change
on what you think you know
is dangerous, but when you reconcile
it with what you know, a clearer
answer begins to emerge.*

"Maybe, maybe not. Let's look at your last promotion and apply the questions. First, what did you know about the new position?"

"I knew the key responsibilities," John began. "I knew where I would be working. I also knew the job offered more money."

"Good enough. Now, what did you *think* you knew?"

John looked out across the fields as he reflected on his response. "That's a little tougher. I guess I thought I knew I could handle the job, that I could be successful with it and that the job would be a good stepping stone for the future."

"Would you have taken the job simply on what you *thought* you knew about the position and yourself without seeing the job description or knowing the pay?"

"Of course not," John replied. "That would have made no sense."

"Exactly," Tara affirmed with a smile. "And what did you not know that convinced you that you should take the job?"

John wanted to argue with her logic, but then slowly smiled as he replied, "I didn't know when the opportunity might come around again or what might happen if I said 'no.'"

"Right!" Tara exclaimed. "It's the same with me and these trees. I don't know if the apples they produce in the next few years will be my best-seller, but they could be. And, I don't want to take the chance of hurting my business because I didn't take the opportunity to change."

Tara stood up to head back to the office. "You know, John, you might actually learn something up here, after all."

John gave a laugh as he started to get up but then felt the stiffness in his back. "I might learn something if all this bending and stooping doesn't kill me first." They got into the truck and headed back to Tara's office.

TARA'S TIPS

Grafting is a process where you take the strengths of two different things and create a better result.

Changing something that is established is rarely easy, but is necessary if you want to get something better.

Always basing your change on what you think you know is dangerous, but when you reconcile it with what you know, a clearer answer begins to emerge.

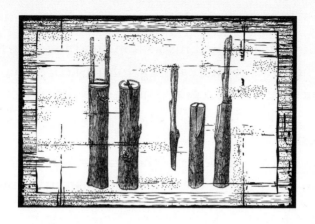

Bringing the Two Pieces Together

While driving back to the office Tara took a different route. "I need to go by to check some grafts Ryan made a few weeks ago and see how they are doing," she said. They soon parked alongside some small trees much like the ones on which they had just been working. Tara and John exited the truck.

As they walked along the row, John noticed that Tara occasionally stopped and closely inspected the grafted area. At one tree she just shook her head and said, "That one will never work."

"Why not?"

Tara pointed to the location of the graft. "Ryan put it facing the West and the afternoon sun has already scorched the small piece of stem. You have to protect the graft to give it every chance to be successful."

They finished their inspection and then returned to the truck. As they were riding, John asked, "Interesting comment about how grafts need to be protected. Are there other things necessary to make sure a graft is successful?"

"Actually," she began, "there are six key things we have to do to ensure the success of the grafting process. I guess you'd like to know those, too?"

"You bet." John opened a notepad in the seat of the truck and began writing.

"First, you have to choose the best method for the graft to be successful," Tara explained. "There are stem grafts, root grafts, budding like you did today, and any number of other methods. Choosing the proper method based on the trees involved is critical.

"Secondly, the timing of the graft is important. We were grafting today because the trees are just beginning to grow and the bark is tender enough to shape around the bud. Six weeks ago the bark would have split.

"The most critical of all the steps comes next and that's lining up the stem and rootstock when they are placed together. The piece of stem that will grow and create the new limbs and the rootstock which will be its roots each have layers that carry nutrients and water up and down the plant. If they aren't lined up correctly, the stem grafted to the rootstock can't survive."

John interrupted her. "So, you can make the right choice, and choose the right time but still experience failure if the new stem doesn't get the nutrients it needs?"

"Yes. Remember that you are changing something that was firmly established in one environment and you are placing it in a different environment."

Tara's response reminded John of his past failure related to reading. He had made the conscious decision at the beginning of the year to read one book a week. The timing was good because the winter months were not as hectic for him as the warmer ones. After a couple of months, though, John abandoned his goal.

Looking back on it now with a new perspective, he saw that he never "lined up" the resources to make the change work. He had tried to read just before bed and kept falling asleep, or he attempted it first thing in the morning when his mind was racing with a million thoughts of the day ahead. He realized that a better option might be taking a few minutes at lunch or after his morning exercise while he was cooling down. His physical and mental resources would be more "in line" with what he was trying to accomplish.

A bump in the road jarred his focus back to Tara. "Okay," he said. "I get the picture with that one. What's next?"

Tara continued. "Fourth is what we just talked about when we were looking at the trees— protecting the graft. Grafting actually occurs naturally with some plants, but of course, nature chooses how and when that happens. Since we are choosing the time to make the change, we have to provide the right environment to help ensure the graft can be successful. Shading is one way. There are others."

"So, once you have done all that, it's just a matter of waiting to see if the graft actually works?" John inquired.

"Not exactly," Tara replied. "Once the new part of the plant begins growing, we have to make adjustments. The stems that were not grafted will also try to grow new limbs, and we have to cut them away so the focus stays on the growth of the new grafted stem. If we don't, the grafted piece is weakened and may not survive."

They arrived at the office and Tara shut off the truck engine as John gathered his things. He looked down at his watch and said, "Wow, where did the day go?"

Tara chuckled and said, "My day is not over."

"I know; mine isn't either. I need to get back and prepare for my meetings tomorrow."

As John opened his car door, Tara asked, "Don't you want to know what the sixth step is?"

In his haste to get ready to leave John had completely forgotten about the last step. He looked at the pad in his hand and frowned. "That's right; you did say there were six, but, looking at this list, what else could there be? We've covered planning, execution and review. It almost sounds like a business plan."

"Yes, but you have to go back to the original reason we started the process, which was to get something better," Tara explained. "If we have done all this planning and work, we'd better make sure the process and the end result were worth it. Simply put, we have to evaluate the success of the graft. If it was about selling more apples, did we sell more apples? If it was about selling the grafted trees, how many trees did we sell? Was it profitable? We have to take time to evaluate the entire procedure to ensure that we have more information for the next change that might be needed."

"You mean so that you have more answers to the question, 'What do I know?'" John said.

"Yes!" Tara responded. "**Evaluating the success or failure of a change gives you more direction when making your next change.** I think one of the reasons we have been so successful here is that we have been willing to try new things, give them every chance to work, and then carefully evaluate the results in relation to our desired outcomes. In other words, always comparing what we have grown by making the change to what we actually *wanted* to grow in the first place."

Evaluating the success or failure of a change gives you more direction when making your next change.

John gently nodded his head in agreement and turned to put the rest of his things in the car. Tara moved around the truck and gave him a quick hug.

"Drive carefully on your way back," she said.

"Oh, I thought I would drive fast and take chances."

Tara groaned in response. "You just never change. It's been so good to see you. I look forward to our next journey into the 'orchard.'"

"After my back recovers from today, I will, too," John replied. He slowly lowered himself into the seat and drove out of the parking lot.

TARA'S TIP

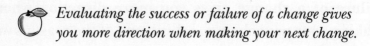

Evaluating the success or failure of a change gives you more direction when making your next change.

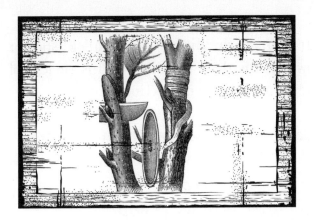

Bringing Out the Tools

The drive back to the hotel gave John a chance to digest his time with Tara and her thoughts on grafting. While the biological side of the process was still pretty much Greek to him, even he could grasp the overall strategy: *Bringing together two elements through a natural process to get a better result.* Grafting was a way to make a change.

Tara's three questions did seem like an effective way to establish the need to change. Determining what was known could reveal the facts surrounding the change. Asking what was *thought* to be known added to the incentive to change or not to change. And, uncovering the things that were *not* known either affirmed the urgency for change or created the need to dig for more answers before engaging in the change. In the past he had allowed the unknown to simply discourage him from taking action.

After an early dinner and quick shower, John sat down at his desk to continue his review of Tara's comments and their connection to change. He wrote:

In deciding if change needs to happen, take stock of the situation by asking yourself three questions:

- What do I <u>know</u>?
- What do I <u>think</u> I know?
- What do I <u>not</u> know?

Answers to these questions will reveal the urgency to change or for things to stay the same.

To best ensure that a change is successful, six things must be done:

- Choose the best method for the change.
- Determine the right timing for the change.
- Line up the layers so that the change has the resources it needs.
- Protect the change to give it every chance to be successful.
- Review progress with the change and make adjustments.
- Evaluate the success of the change in respect to the process and the end result.

John sat back in his chair and reflected on his notes. "Interesting process," he thought. "I wonder if the concept of grafting would work in other situations." Thinking about his team at Trendex, John wondered just how to apply this fresh way of looking at things in order to achieve better results.

His biggest struggle at work was to find a way to improve their overall performance. They were at least a year behind in achieving the same type of results as their counterparts at other sites. He had tried showing them the disparity between their division and other ones, but they just seemed to ignore the facts. Maybe it was because he was seen as the "new kid," or maybe some of them just didn't care. He didn't know for sure. What he *did* know was that the company was counting on him to turn things around, and that he needed to do something, and do it quick.

John decided that when he returned to the corporate office it might be time to practice some "grafting" of his own. He took one more look over his notes and then turned in for the evening.

The morning following his return from Trendex East, John arrived early at the office and set up for his weekly meeting. He was taping his last piece of flip chart paper to the wall when Keith came in the door. Looking at John's drawing he laughed and said, "Need some crayons? I think I have some in my desk drawer."

"Sure, Keith," John replied as he shook his hand, "and bring me some *Play Dough*, too."

Matthew entered the room next and sat down across from Keith about the same time that Chris walked in and took his seat. Laughter could now be heard in the hallway. "Gotta be Luke and Josh," he thought. Sure enough, they both came in the room finishing up a recounting of something that had happened recently at work. Luke noticed the flip charts and drawing and said, "Cool— art class."

Josh took one look and said, "How was your trip to the 'dark side?'" Josh resented any comments John made about how other divisions were outperforming them and took every chance to try to discredit their achievements.

John sighed and said, "Fantastic! You should go with me sometime." Josh rolled his eyes and took a seat next to Keith.

Anxious to get started with the meeting, John realized that, as usual, he lacked one person— Michelle, who was always late. She didn't plan to be late; she just always tried to do "one more thing" before leaving her work area, and if someone wanted to talk to her while she was on the way to a meeting, she would try to briefly talk with them and take care of their issue or concern, putting her even further behind. John looked at his watch one more time and made the decision to begin without her.

Beginning with some general updates about his visit to Trendex East, John was quickly moving through some performance numbers when Michelle rushed through the door. "Sorry," she said. "Nora stopped me in the hall and needed some information about the new marketing plan." She sat down next to Luke and shuffled through her bag looking for a pen. Luke handed her one from the table and she whispered, "Thank you." John nodded in appreciation to Luke and continued with the numbers report. Finishing that, he stood up and moved to his flip chart paper on the wall.

"Having been in this position several months, I think all of you know what Trendex expects of me in my leadership position," he began. "They expect me to bring the results of our division in line with what other divisions are achieving. We've made some progress recently, but we are still not where we need to be, and the clock is ticking. We need to make some bigger changes than the ones we have made so far."

John then turned to the flip chart and hurriedly drew an apple tree. It was clearly out of proportion with a large number of roots but small limbs. He took another marker and then drew three tiny apples growing from a couple of the branches. "Let's imagine for a moment that this apple tree represents our division. How does it look?"

Luke spoke up. "Well, it looks like it has great roots but something is not happening up top."

Matthew added, "It's got a strong foundation but it's not producing much fruit."

"Exactly," John replied. "So, if it's not producing the apples we want, we just need to cut it down, don't we?"

"No!" Chris replied. "If that tree is our division, you have just taken away the jobs of everyone in this room and all the people with whom we work."

"Right, Chris, but if it's not producing the desired results, what other choice do we have?" John shot back.

Josh didn't like where this discussion was headed and said, "And, that's what you have wanted all along, isn't it?"

John could feel the tension rising in the room. "Absolutely not, Josh," John responded, "but, we do have to find a way to grow better apples."

John knew the uncertainty of the moment was exactly what was needed. He wanted them to see the reality of their situation in a different way and to be hungrier for a solution. He picked up a marker and quietly drew a new limb on the tree. He added apples much larger than the existing ones.

As he put the marker down, he asked his team, "What if there were ways to continue to use this tree and get the results we really want? Would that be a better solution?" John could sense a little optimism returning to the group.

"Of course," Michelle replied, "but, you can't just start growing different apples on the same tree." John was ready to reveal his idea when Keith stole the moment.

"Well, actually you can," Keith stated. "My father had a tree that grew five kinds of apples on one tree." Everyone in the room looked at Keith like he was from another planet.

John ended their moment of confusion by saying, "It's called grafting."

John took a few moments to explain what he had done a couple of days ago at Tara's orchard and how he recognized how the application could work in their situation. He even showed them some of the stems from which the grafts were made.

"So you see, grafting is taking two elements with their own individual strengths and creating something better," John explained. "I think it's the same with this division. We aren't in need of being 'cut down,' but I do think we need to graft in some new processes and procedures to help us get better results." A couple members of the group nodded in agreement. He wasn't sure about Josh or Chris.

"Let me be honest," he said slowly. "Change, like grafting, is not an easy process. In fact, a tremendous amount of work goes into creating and nurturing the graft to make it successful.

"Before we begin talking about any possible changes to be made, I think we need to take 'stock' of our situation to make sure change is necessary."

John then divided the team into three groups and had each one of them write their answers to the following three questions as it related to their current situation:

- What do we <u>know</u>?

- What do we <u>think</u> we know?

- What do we <u>not</u> know?

After the groups worked on their responses, John reviewed the flip charts with them. Their answers included the following:

<u>What do we know?</u>

- Productivity in our division is down by 20% compared to other divisions.

- John is the 3rd manager in two years to lead this division.

- There is increased competition in the marketplace for our core products.

<u>What do we think we know?</u>

- Trendex will not allow this division to continue indefinitely with poor performance.

- We could all lose our jobs if we merge with another division.

<u>What do we not know?</u>

- When the economy might change to help the entire company
- How long Trendex will give John and us the opportunity to improve our situation

With this information in front of them, John took a deep breath and asked the question, "So do we need to change?"

"In the worst kind of way," Luke responded. "I'm not crazy about doing things differently, but the alternative is not looking good."

The rest of the team nodded in agreement. John could almost hear his sister saying, "See. It does work."

He picked up a piece of the stem and asked the group, "So what do we need to graft onto our existing tree to make it produce better results?" The group had a lively discussion and came up with a list of improvements needed. Agreed responses ranged from "improved accountability" to "reduction of non-critical meetings" to "more standardized processes and less layers of approvals required for certain requests."

The next step for the group was to identify some of their "roots of strength" that would anchor and support the change. Phrases like "open communication," "honesty" and "willing to work hard" were shared, along with others.

John didn't want to press his luck with his team and go too far in one day. Just getting them to collectively acknowledge that change needed to happen and what needed to happen was a victory, but he knew the *how* of change was going to be the difficult next step to take. John walked to the wall behind Matthew and moved a flip chart page to expose a list he had prepared earlier.

"In the next two weeks I would like to meet with each of you individually to address what changes you and I recognize need to take place for your area. In that meeting we will be using this six step process to determine how to best make the changes successful."

He reviewed the flip chart with the following six questions:

- What is the best method to make the change?
- What is the best timing for the change?
- What are the resources needed to make this change successful?
- How can we protect this change to give it every chance to succeed?
- How often should we review progress with the change and determine any necessary adjustments?
- How will we evaluate the success of the change— both the process and the end result?

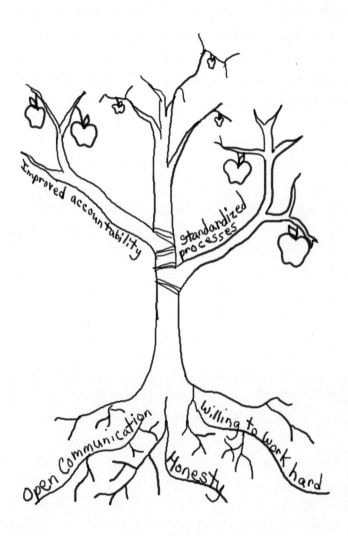

With a few final comments, the meeting ended and his team headed out the door. He wasn't sure if they were in agreement or just shocked by the frankness of the discussion. Either way, John knew it was a step in the right direction. But would everyone want to walk with him through this "orchard?" He would not have to wait long to find out.

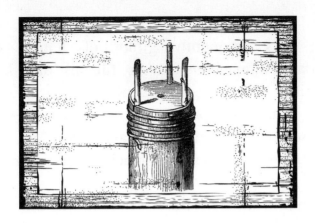

Making the Graft Work

Settling in at his desk a couple days later, John checked his schedule for the day, reviewed new emails for any urgent messages, and then closed the door to his office. The grafting exercise with the rest of his team had gone well, but he knew that he had to do some grafting of his own to improve as a manager. He took out a sheet of paper and began drawing his own "apple tree" with its vast roots and less impressive stems. He chuckled to himself as he drew the small apples that exemplified his current performance in some areas of his work. His roots of strength were labeled with things like "passionate" and "purpose driven".

As he considered what needed to be changed, John recognized that he had to start with how he tackled his big projects at work.

He was frequently guilty of letting crises and daily management tasks fill his day, leaving little time for strategic planning or focus on his team members' performance improvement, so he drew one new grafted limb and labeled it: *Focused Work Hours.* Another was labeled: *Individual Team Member Improvement.*

John continued the process by following the six steps he had outlined earlier, listing answers as needed. The answers were more obvious than he had expected. The best method to achieve more *Focused Work Hours* was to block out time on his schedule for planning. To protect this new time slot, he would need to do a number of things, from sending his calls directly to voice mail to finding a quiet place away from the hustle around his office so that he could actually get the planning done.

For *Individual Team Member Improvement,* John reflected on the upcoming performance reviews and decided that he would incorporate some of the concepts from the grafting exercise into the review. The analogy would help soften the sometimes uncomfortable discussion around areas for performance improvement.

Recognizing he would soon need to leave for a meeting, John reviewed the exercise one more time and listed a couple related items on his task list. He moved the worksheet to a visible part of his desk and started to return a phone call, but a knock at the door interrupted him. He stood up and walked to open the door.

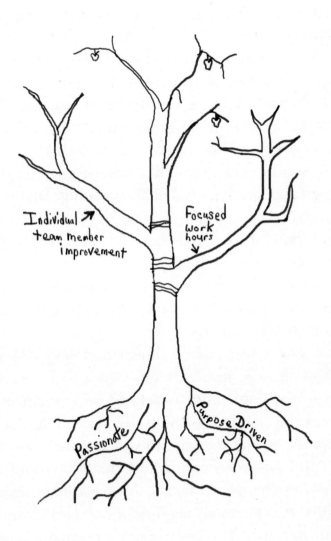

It was Josh. "Why, come in, Josh."

Josh gave a less than enthusiastic smile and moved to a chair at the conference table. John took a place opposite him and asked, "What's up?" knowing Josh rarely popped into his office. Before he spoke, Josh's expression stiffened. He said, "John, I've been thinking a lot about our exercise the other day, and I just don't know if Trendex is the right place for me anymore."

John leaned on the table and said, "What did I do the other day that would make you think that?"

"All this talk of change— like what we are doing just isn't good enough; I'm tired of always being told I need to change."

John thought for a moment and then asked, "Did you complete the exercise?"

"You mean the part about grafting?" he said with a sneer. "Not yet. It's only going to scream at me more about the need to change."

John saw a teachable moment and said, "Maybe there's more to it, Josh." He grabbed a pad from the corner of the conference table and once again drew the tree, and pointed to the roots. "Josh, I apologize if I sent the wrong message to you and the team the other day. I sincerely don't believe that everything you do needs to change. In fact, I think you have several strengths we desperately need right now and will need for years to come." The positive encouragement caused the expression on Josh's face to soften.

John spent the next few minutes helping Josh identify his roots of strength and how they were needed if the division were going to achieve the desired results. Buoyed by the positive conversation, Josh acknowledged some of his own needed "grafts" and gave a couple of thoughts on how he might make the changes successful.

As they finished the discussion, Josh gave a nod to John and said, "John, I apologize if I was a little over the top a few minutes ago."

"No need to apologize, Josh," John said assuringly. "Being candid is one of your roots of strength that I really appreciate. You may have just helped me see another area where some grafting might be needed for me." Josh smiled and walked out of the office.

Returning to his desk, John took a moment to reflect on what had just happened. He knew he didn't want to miss the point himself, so he wrote down in his notepad: **Help others see their roots of strength and how they are needed to achieve award-winning results.**

Flipping back through some of the pages in his pad before he closed it, John stopped at the page about weeds in an orchard and how they can take away resources needed by the tree. As he thought for a moment, John recognized a potential "weed problem" that could develop in his current work orchard. Trying to move everyone along so quickly with change could cause them to think he did not value their current contributions.

John reminded himself to be more intentional about praising each member of his team for things they were doing well, now. After a few more moments of reflection, he set the pad aside and left for his meeting. It would not be the last grafting exercise he would do that day.

Help others see their roots of strength and how they are needed to achieve award-winning results.

Moving to Another Part of the Orchard

After parking his car in his driveway, John took his usual 3-5 minutes to unwind by tossing a tennis ball to his dog and watching him retrieve it. The few moments of reflection helped him transition from work to spending time with his family. As he walked in the back door, he was greeted by his younger daughter Emma, holding Mary, her favorite doll. Giving her a hug, he asked, "How was your day?"

"Good," Emma replied, "but, Ashley and Mommy didn't have a good day."

"Oh, really?" John asked, now looking for Amy. "Why not?"

"I don't know. They just started arguing and Ashley went to her room." John gave Emma a pat on the head and she headed outside to play.

John walked into the study and found Amy at work on her computer. "So, the town crier tells me that all is not well," he commented.

Amy gave him a passing glance before returning to her work. "She just doesn't get it," was her reply. Amy stood up from the desk and hugged John. "Ashley has this academic competition coming up in two weeks and she has hardly prepared for it. There's one part she needs my help with, but every time I ask her about working on it, she's too busy with something else. John, you know how hard she has worked to get to this level. I hate to see her miss out on such a once in a lifetime opportunity."

John nodded in agreement and asked, "Where is she now?"

"In her room," Amy replied. "She stormed up there a few minutes ago."

John smiled and said, "Like mother, like daughter." Amy gave John a half-hearted slap on the arm and smiled in terse agreement.

"Let's go talk to her together," John said.

They walked up the stairs and knocked on her door. "What is it?" was Ashley's response.

John asked, "May we come in for a minute?"

There was a pause and then Ashley said, "I guess so." They opened the door and sat with her on the edge of her bed.

John began: "Your mom tells me that getting ready for the competition is not going so well."

Ashley glared at her mom and then tried to fight back the tears welling up in her eyes. "I just have so many things to do: I've got papers due next week; I've got a piano recital coming up in a few days, and I'm going to be gone to a church retreat all weekend." John gave her a gentle hug as he thought about the visual of Tara's apple trees growing in a hundred different directions and producing a bunch of tiny apples.

"You are probably afraid that you aren't going to do any of them well, aren't you?" John asked.

"Yes," came her muted reply.

John thought for a moment and then said, "Ashley, let's try something. Tell me what you know about everything you have going on in the next few weeks. What are the facts?"

Ashley gave him a look that only a teenager could give a parent and then started. "I have a science project due next Tuesday and a music appreciation project due on Monday. My piano recital is next Thursday and the competition is the week after that on a Wednesday, and I leave this Friday afternoon and won't be back until Sunday afternoon."

"Good," was John's reply. "Now tell me what you *think* you know."

Ashley gave him a blank stare, so he filled in the gaps. "I think I know that if you talked with Ms. Shelton about your science project she would let you turn it in a day or two late; after all, you've worked so hard in her class this year.

"As for your piano recital, I think I know you have the piece 75 percent ready. Sure, it would be good to have it at 100 percent, but this isn't a music demonstration that will determine a college scholarship. It's a chance for you to share your talent, and you will. You might even be able to shorten the piece or choose another one that you already have prepared.

"I also think I know how important this retreat is for you. Kaylee is your best friend and will be graduating this year. The last thing your mom and I want is you stressing out at the retreat and not enjoying time with her."

Ashley had begun to raise her head a little by this point. John then asked the last question: "Now tell me what you don't know about the next few weeks."

Ashley sighed and said, "I don't know if I'll ever get another chance to compete in this competition again."

Amy added, "And, we don't know if your other team members will be coming back next year. They might decide to do other things and that would mean this year is your last year."

Ashley replied, "I know."

"So, with all this information, is it safe to say some things need to change?" John asked.

"Yes," came Ashley's response.

"Good. Let's talk about it more downstairs. I'm starving." He and Amy hugged Ashley and they headed downstairs for dinner.

In between Emma's rambling reports about the day's events, Amy, Ashley, and John worked on how Ashley might improve her situation. She would talk to Ms. Shelton about the science deadline and also look at some other potential recital pieces. They looked at blocks of time she could take to study for the competition, and how they might help her prepare.

As Amy and John cleaned up after dinner, Amy said, "Nice job today, Dad. I've been trying to get her to see things differently for weeks."

"It's a tough life lesson, Amy. One we all have to learn. We often want to give more to the things we *want* to do well in, instead of what we *need* to do well in," John replied. "Thanks for the kudos, but actually my sister's orchard deserves the credit."

"What are you talking about?" Amy replied. As they continued to clean up, John explained more about what he had learned when they were grafting a couple of weeks ago, including the six steps to make a graft successful. They would have continued the conversation but Emma's insistence that they all go play outside stopped them. Remembering his own goal of getting more blue ribbons with Emma, John quickly changed clothes and headed out the door. He didn't know it yet, but the experience with Ashley was preparing him for his next journey into his "orchard."

Cutting Back to Grow Forward

John next visited Tara's orchard in late November. He wasn't exactly sure what he would be doing since the apple growing season was over and the retail store would be the only area in operation.

Walking toward Tara's office, John noticed she was on the phone so he paused at the door. Tara motioned for him to come in so he took a seat at the conference table. Finishing up her call, she came to the table and sat down next to John. "Good to see you, Sis," John said.

"You, too, John."

John noticed the wistful nature in her voice and said, "What's wrong? You aren't your normal chipper self today."

Tara took a deep breath and regained her composure. "Oh, I just got off the phone with another apple grower. Do you remember the trees we grafted earlier this year?"

"You mean the ones you and Ryan grafted and I killed?" John smirked.

Tara grinned and said, "Yeah, those trees. The grower on the phone had heard about my success with the trees and wanted to know if I would consider growing a large quantity for him over the next couple of years."

"Congratulations, Tara," John said. "Another blue ribbon for you!"

"Maybe, but I had to turn him down," Tara replied.

"Why?" John asked.

"My primary purpose in growing the trees was for my own orchard," Tara answered, shifting some papers on the table. "I don't mind selling a few trees from time to time, as well, but I'm just not ready to make that much of a major adjustment in my business plan. I decided it was much better to tell him 'No' now, than to create havoc for myself later."

"In other words," John replied, "You had to say 'No' to something so you could say 'Yes' to something else."

"Almost correct," Tara replied. "Growing award-winning apples has taught me that **you sometimes have to say 'No' to things of lesser importance so you can say 'Yes' to things of greater importance.**

"I could spend my time and energy on a thousand different things, but I wouldn't get a blue ribbon for any of them."

As John reflected on her words, Tara stood up and said, "In fact, I think I can give you a pretty good visual of what I'm talking about while we work today."

"Work?" John replied. "I thought work was over for the season. The apples have been harvested; the vegetables have been sold, and the weather is getting colder. What else is there to do?"

"You still don't get it, do you?" Tara chuckled. She pointed to the quote on the bulletin board which read: *You are growing something every day. What grows and how it grows is up to you.* "Every day I have the opportunity to take actions that will move me closer to the results I want, or move me further away. I choose the former and not the latter, so we need to get to work." John gave Tara one of those "you win but I don't like it" sort of looks and followed her out of the office.

You sometimes have to say 'No'
to things of lesser importance
so you can say 'Yes'
to things of greater importance.

Walking outside, they got into a truck and headed to one of the orchards. After their arrival a few minutes later, Tara rummaged around in the back of the truck.

"Here, hold this," she said as she handed him a three foot step ladder and a pair of hand pruning shears. She got the same items for herself and they walked to the rows and rows of trees in front of them. Setting her ladder down, Tara said, "Today we are pruning."

"Finally! Something I can understand," John said as he moved around to the other side of the tree. "How much do you want me to cut off the top?"

Tara quickly put her hand out and said, "It's not quite that easy."

John frowned and said, "Really? Isn't it just a matter of cutting a few branches at the top?"

"Maybe on a hedge in a landscape, but not in my world," Tara responded as she turned back to the truck. "Let me draw it out for you." She took a pad and pencil out of the truck and sketched a tree. "We have to start by asking what we want the tree to look like two to three years from now. In the case of apple trees, we want to create a tree with five to six main limbs, or stems growing up. From these limbs will grow smaller limbs that will ultimately produce the apples. Apples only grow on wood produced the previous year so if we don't get this pruning done correctly, it has long term consequences."

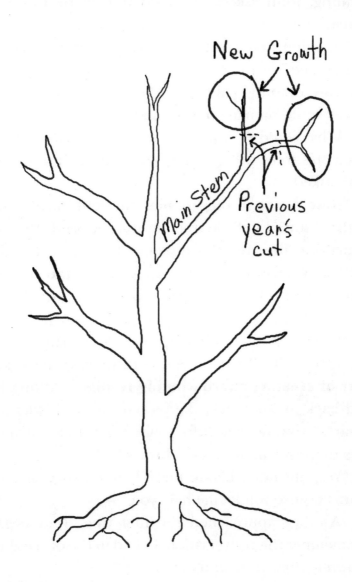

Beginning to sense the complexity of this type of pruning, John asked, "Why do you prune this time of year?"

"Pruning now creates the least amount of danger to the tree," Tara responded. "The cuts on the tree will have time to heal before the cold temperatures of winter could damage the pruned joints."

"Why couldn't you just wait until the summer when the trees are growing and then prune them?" John asked.

"If we prune in the summer, we would waste some of the resources of the tree because we are cutting off something the tree has attempted to grow. Pruning now helps ensure that the resources of the tree are being more efficiently used to create the desired results later."

"You mean blue ribbon apples?" John asked.

"Exactly, Tara responded. **Pruning is a necessary part of creating award-winning results.**" Putting her pad back in the truck, she picked up her ladder and shears. "Now, do you think you're ready to learn about how to prune apple trees?" Tara asked.

"Yes, but don't blame me if you're broke in a few years because you let me help you."

As they approached the first tree, Tara began: "Remember the conversation we had in the office about growing more trees and my saying 'No?'"

"Sure."

Pruning is a necessary part of creating award-winning results.

"Well, let's apply the same reasoning to this tree. How many main limbs or branches do you see?" John stood back for a moment and said, "Six, I think."

"Right," Tara said, "but look over here." She put her hand on a small limb that seemed of little significance to John. "What about this limb? Do you think I need to cut it off?"

"Not really," John replied. "It doesn't seem to be in the way or trying to compete with the other limbs."

"It may not *now*," Tara replied, "but what about as it grows in one year or two years or even three years from now?"

John saw her point and said, "It could be a problem."

"Yes, and what's the advantage of cutting it off now?" Tara asked.

John thought for a moment and said, "We don't waste the resources of the tree on something we really don't want."

"Perfect!" Tara responded. "Now, go back to what I was struggling with in the office. Maybe growing those trees didn't seem like a lot of extra work, but each year it would have required more and more effort on my part.

"The larger I let that area become, the more it would have drawn away resources needed for my core business. By cutting it off now, I minimize the chances for creating an undesirable result. It wasn't an easy decision because the additional income in the short term would be helpful. I just knew it was best for the long term outcomes I have planned for the orchard. Whether it's apple trees, goals or relationships, I have found that pruning is rarely as easy as it seems."

"So it would seem to me that the key to knowing how and what to prune is to be able to envision what you want the results to be in the future after the tree has grown," John stated.

"That's one of the keys, John," Tara responded. "The other two critical things to keep in mind are how to make the best use of the tree's resources and which cuts will stimulate growth in other areas. Remember, **pruning at the right time encourages growth in the areas of greatest importance**."

They looked at a couple of additional trees and then began the actual pruning process. He still had to ask Tara's advice from time to time, but he was gaining confidence in how the process worked. As he approached a tree, he stopped and envisioned what the ideal tree should look like and compared it to the one in front of him. He then analyzed which limbs could be cut and what the resulting tree would look like in one to two years, again comparing it to the desired outcome.

*Pruning at the right time
encourages growth in the areas
of greatest importance.*

As he worked, John frequently created parallels between his own situation and the trees in front of him. At work he had sometimes allowed himself to spend too much time on projects that should have been stopped. He was also guilty of saying "yes" to too many things and while they didn't seem like a "big limb" at the time, they had grown to the point where they were taking resources away from areas that he knew were more important. He could have saved himself a lot of stress and frustration if he had only pruned them earlier.

John also recognized some pruning opportunities at home. He loved working outside with Amy in their flower beds and taking care of the lawn, but he realized that he and Amy might need to cut back on some of the time spent there. Time with Ashley and Emma needed to be a higher priority.

John was painfully reminded of an experience he had a few years ago. He had made a joke about the poor condition of a friend's lawn and the friend responded, "I'm growing children right now. The grass can wait." He now understood the wisdom in that comment.

John decided to find someone else to mow the lawn next year and try to involve the girls in more of their outdoor work.

Moving to another row of trees he thought about his own personal well-being. He resolved that the first "cuts" he would make in this area would be limiting his time watching TV, using the Internet and checking his phone for messages after work. Consciously reducing time spent on these things would help him be "in the moment" more often with his family, as well as give him time to plan how he could achieve a graduate degree.

"And, yes," John thought with a chuckle, "I need to cut out the nighttime snacks." He knew the unhealthy treats frequently eaten late in the evening were reducing the quality of his sleep and causing him to have less energy the next day for work.

The sound of footsteps shook him from his time of reflection. "Nice work, John," Tara began. "We might just have found a new orchard manager."

"Oh no," John replied. "I have no intention of quitting my day job. I'll leave this stuff to the experts."

"Well, good job on what you have done. Let's stop with this row. Ryan and the others will finish up later." John picked up his ladder and they loaded the items in the truck. As they drove toward the office, John smiled as he thought about all he had learned, but he still had one question about pruning that he wanted to ask Tara.

TARA'S TIPS

You sometimes have to say 'No' to things of lesser importance so you can say 'Yes' to things of greater importance.

Pruning is a necessary part of creating award-winning results.

Pruning at the right time encourages growth in the areas of greatest importance.

Timing Is Everything

As Tara drove past an area of the orchard with older trees, John asked Tara to stop. As she pulled the truck to the side of the gravel road, John asked, "Is pruning done the same way with these older trees as the younger ones?"

"Why do you ask?"

"Well," John replied, "I see how important it is to keep the younger trees pruned to encourage one type of growth and discourage another type, but it would seem that if they have been pruned correctly in the early years, the amount of pruning needed to be done as they grew older would be less."

"The answer is 'yes' and 'no,'" Tara replied. **"Pruning in the early stages of growth is most critical because you are forming the structure for the future.**

*Pruning in the early stages of growth
is most critical because you are
forming the structure for the future.*

"If we have done our job correctly, most of our future pruning is spent on removing the dead, damaged, deformed or diseased branches.

"I gave you a 'no' answer as well, though, because sometimes we do have to make large pruning cuts on older, more mature trees. Even though the potential for disease and injury to the tree is much greater with these types of cuts, we sometimes have to do it to try to maintain the overall health and productivity of the tree."

"So, pruning at the right time in the life of the tree is critical, huh?" John asked.

"Absolutely," came Tara's strong reply. "In fact, let's look at another example." She started the truck and they drove to the part of the orchard with the trees they had grafted earlier in the year.

As they walked along the trees, John saw that some of the trees were not showing signs of successful grafts. On other trees, however, the small piece of stem had grown into the existing tree and was creating a new limb.

Tara knelt at one of the trees with a successful graft, pointed to the new branch being created by the graft and said, "See this new stem. It needed the support of the other limbs on this tree to provide food and shading. Now, these new limbs need to become the main stem of this tree. The only way that can be encouraged to happen is to cut back the other limbs on the tree."

"So, pruning too early would have limited your ability to get the results you were looking for, but pruning too late also limits the outcome?" John asked.

"Yes, timing is critical when resources are limited. Timing is also one of the hardest things to teach people who help me manage the orchard. There are three key principles about pruning that if they ever internalize, they are much more effective at getting better results."

"The first is **the faster something is growing, the more often it needs to be examined for the need for pruning.** There is an increased risk of missing a branch that really should have been cut sooner, and now the cut is more dangerous to the tree, and valuable resources have been lost."

The faster something is growing, the more often it needs to be examined for the need for pruning.

"The second principle is to **prune at the first signs of undesirable outcomes.** I can't tell you the number of times I'll be walking through one of the orchards and notice several trees that need some minor pruning. The manager will tell me that they will 'get to it' next week or in a few days. On our next review of that same group of trees, I'll see those trees with larger limbs that now need more major pruning. When I ask about why they haven't taken care of it, they say they were 'just too busy.' It's then I remind them that they are only limiting their ability to get the award-winning results they really want and that I expect."

John immediately connected with Tara's comment about "the first signs of undesirable outcomes." In a previous position he was the accounts manager for a small medical supplies company. He had one client who was consistently unreasonable in his demands. John tried every way possible to make the client happy, but nothing seemed to work. He discussed the issue with his manager early on in the situation, and the manager's response was, "He's a big customer. Make it work."

Prune at the first signs
of undesirable outcomes.

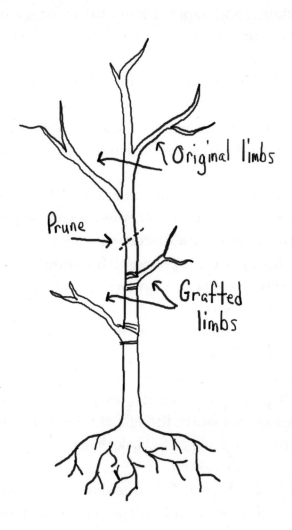

John had tried on a number of future occasions to seek guidance and support from his manager on the issue but continued to get no help. The lack of support eventually caused John to leave the company, and he later heard that the client found another supplier, as well. Had his manager intervened earlier, he might have been able to salvage the customer and even keep John as an employee. John turned his attention back to Tara.

"Lastly," she said, "remember that **while pruning creates future desirable outcomes, a lack of pruning creates future undesirable consequences**."

John chuckled as they moved back toward the truck. "Where were you about six years ago when I needed this lesson on pruning?"

"Oh, I was right here in my little orchard, just relaxing and allowing nature to take its course," Tara responded.

John smiled and stuck his tongue out at Tara. "I know, I know. Seriously, though, this idea of 'pruning' would have been a big help back then."

"How so?" Tara asked.

"Well," John began, "I had taken on way too many things at one time. I had accepted a major project at work that took up a lot of my time. Emma was only one and Amy was saddled with so much between her teaching schedule and keeping things functioning at the house. I was the coach for Ashley's soccer team.

*While pruning creates
future desirable outcomes,
a lack of pruning creates
future undesirable consequences.*

"Dad, as you well know, was failing in health, and if that wasn't enough, I accepted a position on a committee to raise money for a new community park. In orchard terms, I was trying to get a blue ribbon in growing apples, pecans and bananas all at the same time."

"What would you have done differently, knowing what you know now?" Tara asked.

"For starters, I would have paid more attention to how my life was growing out of control and needed some pruning. I ignored signs like more frequent arguments with Amy and Ashley not asking me to do things with her because I was always telling her 'no' due to other commitments. I also started missing some deadlines at work.

"I would also have accepted a more limited role on the park committee and done a better job getting other people to take on responsibilities they were supposed to be carrying out already. Looking back on my situation at work, I would have gone to my boss and sought more guidance and assistance with the project.

"He would have appreciated that because it would have moved things along more quickly and probably gotten better results.

"And..." John's voice trailed off for a moment. He swallowed hard and said, "And, that would have given me more opportunities to spend time with Dad." Tara put her hand on John's hand for a moment as they pulled up at the office. "I just feel like that was a time I wasn't doing anything well, and I still think about it."

"John, you were a great son to Mom and Dad," Tara said softly. "You know that. And, I know the relationship you have with Amy, Emma, and Ashley. Maybe you did make some choices then that you regret now, but the positive thing is that you recognize some ways to improve so that you don't experience those same regrets in the future."

Tara reassuringly patted his shoulder as they exited the truck and walked into the office. After a few more minutes of conversation, he gave her a hug and headed for the airport. It was time for him to do some pruning of his own.

TARA'S TIPS

Pruning in the early stages of growth is most critical because you are forming the structure for the future.

The faster something is growing, the more often it needs to be examined for the need for pruning.

Prune at the first signs of undesirable outcomes.

While pruning creates future desirable outcomes, a lack of pruning creates future undesirable consequences.

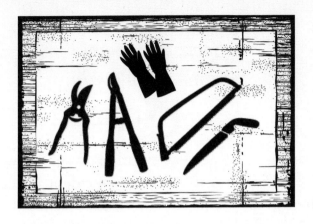

Making the Cuts

John had not expected his time with Tara to be quite so emotionally heavy, but he knew it had once again been valuable in helping him to sort through his own situation. While things weren't growing out of control like they were six years ago, he still knew that some pruning was in order. Ashley had less than one year left at home before she would leave for college. "**Some things you can not grow again,**" he thought to himself. He also needed to get more serious about meeting his goals at work and helping his team members meet theirs.

Those outcomes would require less procrastinating on his part and spending more focused time with them. His twentieth wedding anniversary was also coming up next year, and he needed to start planning their trip. "I can't afford NOT to get a blue ribbon on that one," he said, laughing to himself.

Some things you can not grow again.

Arriving at home that evening, he shared what he had learned with Amy. Since the incident with Ashley and her stress about her overloaded schedule, Amy had taken an additional interest in seeing what, in her words, she could apply to her own "orchard."

John began by showing her his notes about pruning:

- Pruning is a necessary part of creating award-winning results.

- Pruning at the right time increases growth in the areas of greatest importance.

- Pruning in the early stages of growth is most critical because you are forming the structure for the future.

- The faster something is growing, the more often it needs to be examined for the need for pruning.

- Prune at the first signs of undesirable outcomes.

- Pruning creates future desirable outcomes while a lack of pruning creates future undesirable consequences.

John and Amy continued their discussion by talking about some of the "desirable outcomes" they were looking to create or improve. From there, they looked at ways they could prune some items in their schedule. One immediate way they recognized was to delay Emma's entry into playing soccer. They had been considering it, but the extra time spent at practices and games could not be justified now. Ashley would graduate in a year and they could then devote more time to Emma and her athletic development.

Amy also brought up their TV time. They did not watch lots of TV or movies, but had more frequently started using it as something they could all do together. They decided to put limits on how much TV they would watch and instead look at using the time more constructively together. Following their family devotional time the next morning they would make a list of their favorite activities to do together. Each day one family member would be responsible for choosing an activity from the list for them to enjoy.

Amy then mentioned the need to be more conscious about noticing signs of undesirable outcomes. "Give me an example," John replied.

"Okay," Amy began. "How about when you are at home in the evening and your phone gets a new email message and you immediately check it?"

John gave a sheepish grin and then said, "But I don't do that all the time."

"No, but when you do go check it so quickly, it's a sign to me that things are a little out of control for you at work," Amy responded.

"You're right." They spent the next few minutes making a list of other indicators that some pruning might be needed. They included:

- Lack of time for each other
- No opportunities to engage in their personal interests
- Not nurturing relationships with friends
- Being less than patient with the children, especially about little things
- Always arriving late to functions or activities
- Frequently hearing the phrase, "You didn't tell me about that"

After finishing their discussion, John took the first step in doing some pruning in his own personal orchard. He had recently been asked to serve as the chairman for a group raising money for college scholarships for high school students. He had agonized over the decision but realized that saying "yes" to this commitment now would create undesirable outcomes in other areas of his life later.

John called the person who had asked him about serving as chairman. After a few minutes of small talk, he said, "Karen, I really would like to help out right now, but if I said 'yes' to this commitment, I'd have to say 'no' to some other things that are even more important to me." John continued, telling Karen what he *could* give of his time, offering to serve on the selection committee or assist with just one fundraising effort. Karen accepted his offer and told him she would be in contact with him again in a couple of weeks.

As he got off the phone, John's sense of relief was refreshing. Normally, he would have taken the position, struggled to get it done well along with everything else, and ultimately gotten less than stellar results in multiple areas because of overloading his schedule. Now, he had the chance to more critically focus on those areas that needed his greatest attention. "I may actually get a few blue ribbons this year," he thought to himself as he headed off to bed. He would need the rest for what would be coming in the next week.

JOHN'S TIP

 Some things you can not grow again.

One Tree at a Time

Once his family and personal "trees" were in better condition, John turned his attention to his work situation. In his planning time one morning, he made a list of the desirable outcomes he was trying to create, and then thought about some areas of pruning that might be needed to encourage those outcomes. He listed several things, including:

- Limit time reading unnecessary information.

- Stop checking emails as frequently.

- Stop seeing everything as a priority and create three to four "A" priorities per day to accomplish.

- Stop spending time worrying about things that are out of my control and focus on those things that are within my ability to control.

John also took some time to look at the current workload of each member of his team to see if there was anything that could be limited or "cut back" to assist them in better focusing on their most important tasks. His planning would have continued if not for a knock at the door. It was Keith. John stood and spoke to him.

"Hello Keith, good to see you. What can I do for you?"

Keith replied, "If you have a minute, I need to talk with you about something."

"Sure. How may I help?"

"Oh, it's nothing major. I'd just like to talk about the timeline for my retirement. I want to make sure it isn't disruptive to the division," Keith replied.

As they moved to the conference table to sit down, John thought, "Filling Keith's position in the next few months is certainly a 'weed' I need to try to stop in my orchard." Remembering Tara's tip about "preventing the weeds from growing," John tried a different approach.

"Keith," John began, "I hate to break it to you, but losing someone of your caliber will always create disruption in a company. In fact, before we have that discussion, can I ask *you* something?"

"Of course," Keith answered.

"I am in full support of your retirement. Goodness knows you have earned it, but you still seem to enjoy so much of what you do here. If you could sum up your reasons for retirement, what would they be?"

"Oh, I can sum it up in one word," Keith answered.

"Really?" John asked, puzzled. "What word is that?"

"Technology!" Keith responded tersely. "I am fed up with trying to keep up with technology."

John sat back in his chair and thought for a moment. "So, if I could prune some of your responsibilities related to technology, you would consider staying?"

Keith looked off into the distance for a second and then said, "Yes, I think I would. I do love working here and things have certainly gotten better under your leadership."

John thanked Keith for his compliment and spent the next couple of minutes looking at a time to get together again in the next few days to discuss some specific details about helping Keith better manage the technology required in his position.

After the meeting with Keith, John went to Luke's office. He had an idea about how to help Keith. Knocking on his door, Luke called out, "Come in."

John sat down and after a few pleasantries said, "How would you like to have a few more opportunities to work on some technology-related projects?

"I'd love it," Luke responded, "but my plate is full already."

"I know," John said, "but I might be able to help with that, too."

John asked Luke about a couple of meeting possibilities that would line up with his meeting with Keith and he set the meeting date and time before returning to his office.

At the meeting John was pleased to see how receptive Keith and Luke were to working together. It was almost comical. Keith would complain about something he had to do, which related to technology or online tasks, and Luke would say, "Oh, that's easy." A few minutes later Luke would be venting about why something had to be done a certain way, and Keith would give him the background and reasons for the policy or procedure. When the meeting was over, John could see that he had made the right call or "cuts" in this situation. He was encouraging the right outcomes to grow into a reality.

"Maybe we still have a chance to make this division work," John thought. The board of directors meeting was coming up in a few months, and he knew that they still were not quite in line for a blue ribbon, but he was feeling more optimistic all the time.

"I disagree. We have several successfully grafted trees to use for next year. I also have more knowledge about what works and what doesn't work when it comes to grafting these types of apple trees."

John wanted to argue with Tara's overly optimistic attitude, but her results over the past twenty years spoke for themselves. She was one of the most successful apple growers in the region and was operating a financially sound business. Her employees loved working for her company and her family adored her. Most importantly, you could tell that she had a passion for life that few others could match.

Sensing John's pessimism, Tara said, "Let's look at it another way. Think about Linda, the lady you met a few minutes ago. What's the value in having a customer who has come back to my orchard for over twenty years to buy apples? Sure, she may only buy a bushel each year, but I need to celebrate the fact that I grow a quality product that people want to buy and that I have someone telling others about her positive experiences here."

They drove to another part of the orchard where crews were picking apples and joined the group. John grabbed one of the cloth bags, placed it over his shoulder, climbed a ladder and began picking, as well. He was lost in thought about Tara's comments—*Harvest is the season when you look at your productive results.*

John was a little disappointed in himself for not having a "harvest" attitude more often. He was always beating himself up about not being the dad he wanted to be or not hitting the numbers for his division for the quarter. He rarely took the time to look at what he was doing well. He now realized that his limited perspective was one of the reasons he didn't have the motivation to work on improvement of other areas of his work and life.

John stepped down from the ladder and unloaded his bag of apples into one of the wooden crates. Tara came over to join him and they started working on another tree. "Sorry I wasn't here to help with that last tree," she said. "I was talking with one of the workers about the new addition to their family."

"That's okay, Tara," John responded. "I would imagine you consider that part of your harvest as well."

"Absolutely," she replied. "In what other job could I get to do the things I like to do so much— grow apples and talk with people?"

Her comments made John think about his own job situation. "Speaking of jobs, I may need to join you soon if things don't improve for me."

"The board of directors meets soon, huh?" Tara asked.

"Yes, and I just don't know if we have done enough to keep the division going," John replied. "That would be the harvest for us."

"Well, there's a way to find out if you have done enough," Tara responded.

"I know. After the board meeting," John said.

"No, I mean <u>right now</u>," Tara answered.

"Be serious," John said. "You really do have your head in the clouds, sometimes, you know."

"Maybe, but I'm not the one worried about having to go to work for his sister," Tara said with a chuckle.

"Okay," John replied. "Let's hear it."

Tara began. "You already know my favorite quote: *You are growing something every day.* For years that one phrase helped me to be intentional about what I would work on every day, primarily growing award-winning apples. However, I soon began to notice that just focusing on the growing side of things blinded me to what I was actually achieving, or 'harvesting,' if you will— strong relationships with others, good health, financial security, and service to the community. It was only when I learned to more frequently reflect on the results of my efforts that I could more clearly appreciate the results and determine what I might need to work on growing tomorrow. Evaluating your harvest helps determine what you need to grow in the future."

"So how does that help me know if I have done everything to be successful with my division?" John asked.

"Simple," Tara replied. "Ask yourself three questions:

- What did I do to create the environment for the right things to grow?

- What new ideas, attitudes or actions did I graft into my work that brought better results to me, as well as others?

- How did I prune poor ideas, attitudes or actions out of my work so that more of the right things were encouraged to grow for me and others?

If you have some specific answers to these three questions, you are well on your way to getting award-winning results, whether it is at work, with your family or your own personal well-being."

John thought for a moment as he was getting off the ladder. "It goes back to being intentional doesn't it?" he asked.

"Sure does. **You have to be as intentional about analyzing your harvest as you do determining what you are choosing to grow.** If they don't match up, something needs to change."

Picking the last apples from the tree, John and Tara placed them in the crate. John asked, "Isn't it about lunch time?"

"You are surrounded by some of the tastiest apples in the world," Tara answered. "What could be better than that?"

*You have to be as intentional
about analyzing your harvest
as you do determining
what you are choosing to grow.*

John laughed as he picked an apple out of the crate and got into the truck. "I'll consider this my 'apple¬tizer,'" he said. Tara gave a deep sigh as they drove back toward the office and John bit into the large red apple.

"Yes," came Tara's reply, "if you know you have done all you reasonably can do to get the award-winning results you are looking for. It goes back to those three questions I just mentioned."

Driving up to the office, John and Tara stepped out of the truck, washed their hands and got their sandwiches out of Tara's office. After stopping for a few minutes for Tara to talk with some customers, they walked out behind the old barn and sat down at a picnic table.

As they were eating lunch, John said, "If I understand all this 'orchard speak' correctly, I think I hear you telling me that effort should be rewarded and not just achievement."

"You bet. **An award-winning effort doesn't always result in a blue ribbon.** I've had years where we worked really hard growing, grafting, and pruning. We did everything possible to grow the best apples, but due to the weather or the economy or something else out of our control, we just didn't get the results we were looking for. That doesn't mean the individuals and the efforts they put forth should not be recognized in some way.

"In fact, I've found that when it comes to working in a business, **if you only reward individuals when the team gets a blue ribbon, people lose the motivation to try to accomplish very much at all.**" Tara motioned to the line of trees that she had let grow out of control many years ago. "It's like those trees. If I had let myself get discouraged because those trees didn't turn out perfectly, I would have never gotten to the place I am today. Thankfully, Grandpa was the one who encouraged me to keep trying and took the time to show me where I did some things right and how I could improve next time."

An award-winning effort doesn't always result in a blue ribbon.

If you only reward individuals
when the team gets a blue ribbon,
people lose the motivation to try to
accomplish very much at all.

Even though Tara was talking about a team in work terms, John recognized the correlation of her comments to his "family team." One of the blue ribbon results they sought as a family was providing encouragement to individuals who were facing difficulties of one kind or another. They sometimes prepared meals or a dessert to give to other people or took care of something they needed done around their home. Other times they picked flowers and made simple arrangements to brighten someone's day. Emma often designed cards with her own personal drawings and they mailed them to others, as needed.

With their crazy schedules over the past few months, he and his family had not been as disciplined with their acts of kindness as they should be. John had even expressed his disappointment to his family on several occasions. Hearing Tara's comments reminded him that he should be doing more praising of what they were doing instead of frequently expressing concern over what they were not doing.

As they finished their lunch, John knew it was time for him to head to the airport. As Tara walked with him to his car, she said, "John, let me ask you one more thing."

"Sure," John replied. "I'm normally the one asking all the questions."

"Are you a better person than you were two years ago?" she asked.

John had not expected that kind of question and he was even more surprised at his almost automatic response of "Yes."

"How so?" Tara inquired further.

"Well, at work I am certainly more focused on my outcomes and spend more time helping each member of my team accomplish his goals."

"Good," Tara replied. "Anything else?"

"My relationship with Amy has improved since we have become more intentional about creating the right environment for us to grow as a couple and with our girls."

"But have you seen any improvement in yourself, your own personal well-being?" Tara asked.

John had to think for a moment, but then said, "I'm definitely more proactive when it comes to seeing the need to change and making better choices." He gave Tara a "muscle man" stance and said, "I'm certainly in better physical shape. I had my best time ever in my last 5K event."

"Then I'd say that's a pretty good harvest for two years, wouldn't you?" Tara asked.

John now saw her point even more clearly as he said, "You're right. I need to celebrate more of the things I *have* accomplished instead of the two or three things I *haven't* accomplished."

"Exactly," Tara responded, putting her hand on his shoulder.

As John got into the car he looked at Tara and said, "Thanks."

"My pleasure," she said warmly. "It's what 'know it all' big sisters are supposed to do for their little brothers." John gave her one last smile, cranked the engine and closed the door.

TARA'S TIPS

The harvest is about much more than just the numbers.

Harvest is the season when you look at your productive results.

You have to be as intentional about analyzing your harvest as you do determining what you are choosing to grow.

An award-winning effort doesn't always result in a blue ribbon.

If you only reward individuals when the team gets a blue ribbon, people lose the motivation to try to accomplish very much at all.

A Celebration

John was a little more tense than normal. The board of directors was meeting in just over a week and the anxiety of not knowing the outcome lay heavy on his mind. "We have worked so hard," he thought to himself. "The board just has to see that."

Tara's words had been of some comfort as he looked ahead to next week. He now knew there was some celebration of his team's harvest they needed to have as a division before they got the official answer. He called Amy and asked her if they could have a party at the house on Saturday or Sunday night. Getting her agreement, John made contact with everyone on his team and checked their schedules. Saturday night would work for everyone.

On Saturday evening people began arriving with their spouses or dates. They were perplexed by a sign John had put on his porch which read, *Welcome to the Harvest Celebration*. They had no idea what he was implying.

After dinner, John had the group gather in his basement. With everyone seated in a loose circle formation, John began. "I'd like to officially welcome all of you to our harvest celebration."

Luke, never one to hold back, spoke up and said, "Don't you mean our going away party?"

John quickly responded with, "No. If we need to have one of those in a few weeks we can do that, too. What I want tonight to be is a celebration of the productive results we have achieved over the past two years: To share what we have 'harvested' from our efforts together."

John then brought out a flip chart with three questions:

- What have you done to create the environment for the right things to grow at work?

- What new ideas, attitudes or actions have you grafted into your work that has brought better results?

- How have you pruned poor ideas, attitudes or actions out of your work so that more of the right things were encouraged to grow?

John gave his answers to the questions and then invited others to respond. Answers were slow at first, but as people became more comfortable with the exercise the responses flowed more freely. Chris' major change was to set clear expectations for his direct reports, and then follow up. For Keith it was pruning his poor attitude about technology and how that allowed him to work more effectively with Luke. Michelle was the last to offer her thoughts.

"For me," she began, "my biggest achievement has been recognizing that if I try to do everything well, I will do nothing well. I've learned that I have to be more intentional about what I want to excel at and plan my schedule accordingly."

John made a few wrap up comments and finished by saying, "Regardless of what happens next week, I want you to know that in my mind you certainly have achieved award-winning results, and as one symbol of my appreciation, I have a basket of my sister's blue ribbon apples for each of you." The group talked informally for a while and then began dispersing. As the last person left, John and Amy returned to the basement.

"That was a worthwhile thing you did tonight," Amy began. "I think you needed it as much as they did."

"You are exactly right," John responded. "I just wanted them to know how much I appreciated their efforts instead of simply offering them condolences if things don't turn out the way we hope next week."

Pausing for a moment, Amy said, "I've noticed a difference in you around here, as well."

Stopping his work of putting away chairs he said, "How so?"

"Just little things," she responded. "The way you are more focused on doing three things well instead of attempting to do seven things not so well. Take last Saturday. The yard needed work, you had shelves to put up, Danny wanted your help with his computer, and Emma and Ashley were vying for your attention, as well. The old John would have raced around trying to get everything done and wound up frustrated, exhausted and left with more things to 'do over' because of the rush. Instead, I saw you pick just a few things and do them well."

"Let's just say I've learned to be choosier about what I want to get a blue ribbon for," John responded.

"Whatever it is, keep doing it," she responded. "In fact, why don't you work at getting a 'blue ribbon' in kitchen cleanup?"

"I guess," John replied sheepishly. They finished putting away the chairs and went upstairs.

A Change
in the Orchard

The party on Saturday night had done much to boost morale, but there was no denying that people were still feeling anxious about the meeting that was taking place this week. John tried to keep things moving along as normal. In their weekly division meeting he intentionally brought up some elements of their three year strategic plan so they would look beyond this week. The last thing he wanted was for them to take things this far and then let up at the end. "Getting a blue ribbon means that you have earned it every step of the way," he thought to himself.

Personally, John spent some time reviewing his notes from his visits with Tara. He had learned so much about growing apples, but more importantly about himself.

John better understood that getting award-winning results required making some difficult choices, but that the end results or "harvest," as he now called it, was worth the effort. Even more importantly, he had formulated a plan that would help him succeed at work and in his personal life, regardless of the outcome of this week.

The board of directors meeting ended on Wednesday and John knew that Thursday would bring the news. Walking into the building on Thursday morning, he was surprised to find every member of his team absent from their offices. He thought to himself: "A possible sign of things to come."

Later that morning, Matthew was in John's office when the phone rang. Normally he would not answer it, but when the name "Dan Johnson" appeared, he knew he needed to take the call. Dan was one of the executive vice presidents at Trendex and had been a big advocate of seeing John appointed to his current position in the company. He picked up the handset.

"Good morning, Dan Johnson," John said.

"Good morning, John," Dan replied. After a couple of superficial comments, Dan got to the point. "John, I'd like to meet with you for a few minutes today if that's possible."

"Sure," came John's reply. "How about 1pm?"

"Perfect," Dan answered. "I'll see you, then."

John hung up the phone, mentioned the meeting to Matthew and finished his discussion with him. While the meeting was not a surprise, John felt the anxiety building again. The numbers didn't lie. His division was still behind in productivity compared to other similar divisions. Given time they could definitely get some award-winning results, but there was no pruning, grafting or pixie dust that would get them there more quickly.

John spent his lunch time reviewing his previous reports and rehearsing his comments. Walking out of his office and up the stairs he tried to relax. "Well, at least if I lose my job at Trendex, I can go work with Tara at the orchard," he thought, but the joke did little to calm his nerves. He turned left off the stairs and let Dan's assistant know he was there for the meeting. She told him to go into the room. Taking a deep breath, he opened the door.

To his surprise, John wasn't the only one invited to the meeting. In the room was his entire team: Keith, Chris, Luke, Josh, Michelle and Matthew. John's fears were now at full throttle because he knew the reason for the meeting— his division was being cut. John appreciated that Dan did not leave him to tell his team members, but he would have liked to have a little more prior notice. Shaking hands with Dan and acknowledging the others, John took a seat.

Dan began: "I appreciate all of you taking time to meet with me today. I'll keep this brief because I realize you have a lot going on. As you know, there has been much discussion about whether we should keep your division or not in light of the lack of results we have seen in the past. John was appointed division head in hopes of turning things around. At our board of directors meeting this week we took a long hard look at your current results."

John could feel his face reddening; he looked around the room at the other members of their team and the expressions on their faces were similar.

Dan continued: "At this point, we have only one choice..."

Before he could finish, John interrupted and said, "Dan, may I say something first?"

"Sure, John."

"Please know that it's not their fault," he began. "These are fantastic people to work with. They just needed more time or a better leader. I accept full responsibility for our results."

"That's very noble, John," Dan responded, "but I think you need to give some credit to your team members for the— what's the word— 'harvest' you are experiencing."

"Harvest? Yes, of course, but...." John struggled to make sense of what Dan had just said. "Aren't you going to..."

Dan finished his statement: "...to cut your division?"

"Yes," was John's feeble reply.

"Of course not!" Dan answered. Immediately his team members began laughing and clapping.

"We finally pulled one over on YOU, John," Luke yelled.

"Yeah," Josh answered. "I was glad Dan got to the point. I thought you were going to pass out on us." John smiled and just lowered his head, overwhelmed by the moment.

"My purpose today," Dan continued, "was to congratulate all of you on your extraordinary efforts. You have lived under a tremendous amount of stress for quite a while and I'm thrilled to see how things have turned around. In fact, I was so interested in how you accomplished it that I went straight to the experts for the answers."

Dan got up and walked to a flip chart and easel in one corner of the room. Turning back the first page, he revealed a page with a triangle with four words written on it. At the bottom was the word *Growing.* Next was *Grafting,* followed by *Pruning,* and finally, *Harvest.* Above the triangle was the phrase— *Getting the Blue Ribbon.*

"But how did you know about. . .?" John asked.

"Let's just say I had a meeting with some pretty good apple growers this morning," Dan replied as he looked at John's team members. Now, it all made sense! No one was in their offices earlier today because they were meeting with Dan.

John made eye contact with Matthew. "YOU!" he said. "You were in my office and didn't mention a thing about it."

Matthew simply smiled and said, "And, miss the moment we just had? The look on your face was priceless."

John couldn't stop shaking his head in disbelief. They had done it! They had gotten the award-winning results. Dan continued the meeting, giving some additional feedback from the board and again congratulating them on their achievement. As they prepared to leave, Dan asked John to stay for another minute.

Shaking John's hand, he said, "John, I knew you were the person to lead this team, and after talking with your team members this morning, I would have known that even if the board had made a different decision. They didn't, and now it's time to move forward."

"Thanks for your support, Dan," John replied. "It has been quite a journey."

"Speaking of journey," Dan continued. "One thing the board has requested is that you no longer be required to visit Trendex East to monitor their work. We need you here to continue to improve your division."

While John was elated to hear that he wouldn't have to be on the road as much, he also wistfully knew that the frequent visits to Tara's orchard would no longer be a part of his routine. John thanked Dan again and headed out the door.

Taking a moment for himself, John walked down the steps, out the front door of the building and took a deep breath. "Yes!" he thought to himself. "This is what getting the blue ribbon feels like." He took out his phone and called Amy to share the news. She was thrilled. "Sounds like someone owes a phone call to his sister," she said jokingly as they finished their conversation. "She was next on my list," John said.

John dialed Tara's mobile number and she answered, "Well, hello, little brother! Are you calling to apply for a job at my orchard?"

John replied, "As tempting as that sounds, I think I'll just be content to stay here and run one of the blue ribbon divisions at Trendex."

Tara gave out a yell and said, "We will miss you as an employee but will still look forward to seeing you as cheap labor every now and then."

John's excitement dipped for a moment. He replied, "Actually, one of the results of my success is that I don't have to travel to Trendex East every few months; I get to stay here and focus on one division instead of two."

There was silence on the line for a moment, and then Tara spoke up. "Well, speaking as an award-winning apple grower, I would say that you still have a lot to learn. You have only seen a few elements of the business. If Trendex thinks you have been successful with what you know *now*, just think of what you could do at that company if you had more lessons over the next few years."

John could hear the sarcasm in her voice, but he knew she was right on several levels. If he had been able to make so many improvements based on observations from just a few visits, how much more could he accomplish if he had more time working in the orchard? He also had found the time with her as a family member had been priceless. Work may have been the catalyst to build a stronger relationship, but much deeper bonds would encourage it to continue to grow.

"Well, if you are offering to continue these lessons, I might be able to find a way to get to your orchard from time to time, especially if you could have some of that world-famous apple crumble waiting for me."

"It's a deal, John," Tara replied. "Now if you will excuse me, I need to get to my afternoon nap and allow nature to take its course in the orchard."

"Ha, ha," John replied. "Thanks again, Tara." John ended the call and headed back up to his office, and this time there would be no question about how long he would be there.

A Blue Ribbon Life Indeed

Several years had passed since the day John got his first big blue ribbon at Trendex, but it was certainly not the last one. He received several additional promotions, but he was always careful to evaluate them on how it would affect his continuing desire to get the "blue ribbon" in respect to his relationship with Amy and his daughters, as well as his own personal welfare.

Ashley went to college and became a wildlife biologist. Having spent a considerable amount of time with her Aunt Tara, Emma became interested in plants and gardening and was starting her own fruit and vegetable business.

Making good on his promise, John did visit Tara more often. He was amazed that each time he went, he learned something new. In fact, his coworkers at Trendex gave him lots of grief about his sister being the real brains in his family. On a couple of occasions he brought Tara to Trendex to talk with a new management team or to guide a group through the four strategies of growing, grafting, pruning and harvesting. People said the simple analogy really helped them visualize what needed to be done.

One day when he and Amy drove up to Tara's place, John noticed Tara talking with a group of people. Amy went inside the store to check out what was new, and John walked to where the group was meeting. They were just finishing up when Tara saw John.

"You're too late, the tour is over," she said as she hugged John.

"Tour?" he asked. "Since when do you give tours?"

"Since I realized that people need to hear my story," she replied. "Just like you several years ago, they may be struggling with something at work or life and need a simple way to see what needs to be done, and don't forget, I love to talk with people."

"I see," John replied. "And, if they have questions, do you answer them?"

"Sure," Tara answered.

"Good," John said. "My question is this: 'At what point do you STOP trying to get the blue ribbon?' You have certainly reached a point in life where you could stop working so hard."

"Never," was Tara's quick reply. "**Getting the blue ribbon is not just a one time event. It's a lifelong way of managing your work and life.**"

"So," John continued. "You are telling me that whether I am five or ninety-five that I need to be intentional about making good choices and getting award-winning results?"

"Exactly," Tara replied, beginning to walk. "Let's revisit something."

Tara and John walked past the spot where their grandfather's old barn had once stood. A newer one had taken its place. They stopped where the row of overgrown apple trees had once stood. Only one remained now.

"Remember all those trees that were once in this row?" Tara asked.

"Sure."

Getting the blue ribbon is not just a one time event. It's a lifelong way of managing your work and life.

"Imagine all the apples they could have produced if they had been given the right environment for growth," she said wistfully. "If other varieties of apple trees had been grafted onto their once vibrant limbs— if they had been pruned properly— think about the results they could have had, but, because I lost sight of them for a little while, they were practically useless. No one benefited from their lackluster results.

"You see, **when you stop focusing on getting the blue ribbon, you can miss the opportunity to produce some incredible results.** In my case I chose apples and nurturing strong relationships with people. The blue ribbon for others might be building a successful business where employees look forward to coming to work. Still others might inspire students in the classroom or develop a cure for a disease or simply be the best spouse or parent they can be. You just never know how people can possibly benefit from the award-winning results you try to achieve."

*When you stop focusing
on getting the blue ribbon,
you can miss the opportunity to
produce some incredible results.*

As they turned to walk back toward the office, John smiled at Tara. Her tan face and strong smile still showed the exuberance of the little girl who, at an early age, found a way to get what she wanted out of work and life. John was glad he had found his way, too, even if he did have to give some of the credit to his big sister.

TARA'S TIPS

Getting the blue ribbon is not just a one-time event. It's a lifelong way of managing your work and life.

When you stop focusing on getting the blue ribbon, you can miss the opportunity to produce some incredible results.

It's Time To Start Getting More Blue Ribbon Results!

Getting Your Own Blue Ribbon

You are growing something every day.
What grows and how it grows is up to you.

At the end of each day ask yourself:

- What did I grow today?

- Will I like the result of what I grew today?

GROWING

Trees will attempt to grow in almost any environment

To build the best environment for growth:

- Determine the ideal environment.

- Evaluate current conditions for resources that exist.

- Provide the right combination of nutrients.

The same environment that creates opportunities
for optimum growth also creates the ideal
environment for weeds to grow.

GRAFTING

*Grafting is a process where you take the strengths
of two different things and create a better result.*

**When attempting to decide if change needs to happen,
take stock of the situation by asking three questions:**

- What do I know?
- What do I think I know?
- What do I not know?

**To best ensure that a change is successful, six things
must be done:**

- Choose the best method for the change.
- Determine the right timing for the change.
- Line up ideas with actions so that the change has the resources it needs.
- Protect the change to give it every chance to be successful.
- Review progress with the change and make adjustments.
- Evaluate the success of the change, including the process and the end result, in light of your desired outcomes.

*Help others see their roots of strength and how they
are needed to achieve award-winning results.*

PRUNING

*Pruning is a necessary part of creating
award-winning results.*

The key to knowing how and what to prune is to be able to envision what you want the results to be in the future.

Three Principles of Pruning:

- The faster something is growing, the more often it needs to be examined for the need for pruning.
- Prune at the first signs of undesirable outcomes.
- While pruning creates future desirable outcomes, a lack of pruning creates future undesirable consequences.

You sometimes have to say "No" to things of lesser importance so that you can say "Yes" to things of greater importance.

HARVEST

Harvest is the season when you
look at all your productive results.

To evaluate your harvest, ask yourself:

- What did I do to create the environment for the right things to grow?

- What new ideas, attitudes or actions did I graft into my work or life that brought better results for me, as well as others?

- How did I prune poor ideas, attitudes or actions so that more of the right things were encouraged to grow for me and others?

- Did I achieve the results I was looking for?

An award-winning effort
doesn't always result in a blue ribbon.

Getting the blue ribbon is not just a one-time event.
It's a lifelong way to manage your work and life.

When you stop focusing on getting the blue ribbon,
you can miss the opportunity to produce
some incredible results.

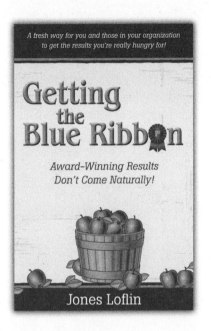

Help Others Get Their Blue Ribbons!

To learn more about:

- Ordering multiple copies of *Getting the Blue Ribbon*
- Keynotes
- Training
- Other products or services

Visit: www.**yourblueribbon**.com
Or call: **1-800-853-4676**